369 ManifeSting Journal

Discover the Secrets to Manifest Your Dream Life

*Learn How to Harness the Power
of the Law of Attraction and Many
Other Methods Through Guided
Techniques and Exercises*

**By:
Bob Barrett**

TABLE OF CONTENTS

Introduction

The world reflects our thoughts, feelings, and behaviors. "The universe is simply the mountain; the echo relies on you," poet Rumi stated. We live in a vibrational environment, and you may tune into the spectrum or 'radio station' of your aspirations.

When we terminated an eight-year relationship with a person who was not suited for us, we began to shift our attitudes and energies toward the opposite sex and relationships. We began to recognize our values and align ourselves with the person we desired to be. We began to suddenly encounter the most fantastic people; it was as if we were in a parallel realm where they were plentiful.

Our brain is a goal-oriented system that filters the outside environment through our main beliefs. So, suppose you've got a dream for your life or think that fantastic possibilities, loving partners, ideal careers, and unlimited prosperity abound. In that case, your mind will begin to provide thoughts and knowledge to help you achieve that goal.

The be-do-have concept dictates that we behave in line with our identity. To achieve our wants with more ease and elegance, we must embody (think, feel, and behave) like the type of people who already possess them. We may begin to express much of that characteristic in the world if we dare to assert, "I am strong, I am innovative, I am great."

If we wish to co-create our aspirations and desires, it all begins within ourselves. It all starts with self-awareness, focusing on discovering and deciding what you believe, actively picking your vibe and energy, and prioritizing synchronization.

"The Universe supports us in any notion we want to conceive and think," Louise Hays remarked. "Whatever we decide to assume, our subconscious mind adapts. They both imply that what I think of myself and my life is fulfilled in my existence."

The universe streams to and through us if we're in tune. As a result, we will experience increased synchronicity and opportunity and inspire our intuitive prompts to act to co-create our wishes.

It does not imply that we must be flawless or that everything is flawless. I'm still experiencing a rainbow of emotions, and we must sometimes feel our sentiments before we can alter them. On the other hand, we may empower ourselves by upgrading our thoughts and energy.

It's more than optimistic thinking when it comes to manifesting — it's about intentionally selecting who you are now. It's about realizing that your ideas impact your emotions, which impacts your behaviors and the lifestyle you co-create.

The delight of being more engaged with your inner consciousness and intuition, the value of harmony or appreciating the process, and how to transcend old tales that no longer benefit you are all benefits that manifestation can teach you.

Practicing alignment may lead to more synchronicity, guidance, and miracles.

"Every minute of our lives provides us a chance to tune into the inventive energy of the world and experience outrageously fantastic synchronicity and connection," Gabrielle Bernstein stated.

Chapter 1: Nitty GrittieS of ManifeStation

Have you often pondered what manifestation is all about? It is a question I am frequently asked as a life coach.

I offer you an overview of manifestation and the Law of Attraction in this book.

This chapter will provide you with some views into the concepts of thinking, metaphysics, and manifestation whether you are a manifesting king or a novice to the subject and want to learn more.

This chapter's goal is to enable you to co-create your dreams with the higher self and the universe and assist you in aligning yourself so that you may feel more synchronization and connectivity.

1.1 Concept of Manifestation

The "law of attraction," or the belief that you gain whatever you set out into the world, underpins manifesting. (Did a relative ever tell you as a kid, "You'll catch more flies with sugar syrup instead of vinegar?") It's a little like that.

Using your thinking patterns, mentality, and self-beliefs to acquire what you desire is what manifesting is all about. Your ideas and beliefs have an enormous influence on your world. The way you perceive might keep you back if you're pessimistic or focused on the problems.

However, changing your mindset to be more optimistic may assist you in moving forward in remarkable ways. Manifestation is the act of harnessing the power of your imagination and ideas to bring something into being that you genuinely desire. Yes, that sounds a little enchanted, but, guess what: You have the power to create magic! You have the strength within you, just as Dorothy in The Wizard of Oz. With this skill, you can do wonderful things, from locating the best parking place in the lotto, landing your ideal dream job, to discovering the soulmate for your life. It's all in your head. The trick is to understand how to harness the power of thought management, appreciate what you presently have, and never give up. If you're having trouble swallowing this, remember that Conor McGregor, Louise Hay, Jim Carrey, Oprah Winfrey, and Jennifer Lopez have all officially acknowledged the Law of Attraction and how manifestation has changed their lives. They all possess one factor in common: they never gave up after putting in the effort. Choosing to leap in with both feet and shift your life to one of prosperity, pure joy, and true fulfillment may be the easiest and most difficult task you will ever do. You, on the other hand, are capable of completing the task.

In its most elementary type, manifestation needs setting your wish for anything you intend to occur and then witnessing it emerge in the real world. All this means that if you trust something, it will happen. Of course, it's a little more complicated. Natalia Benson, an empowering coach for women and astrologer who employs manifestation with clients, adds, "I prefer to think about manifestation as just a fancy phrase for being a dynamic force in your own life." She defines manifestation as "shaping your life the means you intend it to be."

According to Benson, we are constantly manifesting and generating in our worlds, but only subconsciously. As we become aware of our power, we must design our lives as we want them to be lived; here is where manifestation comes from. "When we become conscious enough to admit: it is something I'd want to feel in my life," Benson continues, "it's incredibly powerful." "Let's assume it's a job, a relationship, a sum of money, or a physical sensation. Understanding what you desire for your own experience of life and then visualizing those consequences is what manifesting is all about."

1.2 Five Specific Points About Manifestations

Do you want to give manifestation a shot? Here's what experts advise you should know about manifesting.

1. Spirituality and Manifestation May Go Hand-in-Hand

It's good to know as a novice to manifestation that it's frequently paired with a different kind of spirituality and devoutness, which makes perfect sense once you consider it. "They both have a means of relating us with ourselves," says Ellen Bowles, creator of The Woke Mystix, and Imani Quinn, intuitive.

There are several techniques to do this, but numerous manifesting experts recommend setting intentions or becoming obvious regarding what you intend to occur in the future (think: a pay raise, a new house, or good bonding with the parents).

"The new moon is a great time to set intentions; it's the perfect moment to cultivate new seeds," Bowles and Quinn said. It is only one example of how manifestation might collide with other techniques in this place.

2. There's a Lot More to It Than the Secret

Because of The Secret, a book and movie on the Law of Attraction, many people are acquainted with manifestation. The concept is straightforward: like attracts like. As a result, whatever energy you send out into the world will return to you. If you concentrate on the bad, you will get unfavorable experiences. You'll put yourself in a position for more pleasant events if you maintain a "high vibration" condition.

However, according to manifestation experts, 11 other rules govern how the cosmos operates. According to Benson, the Law of Attraction is only the tip of the iceberg.

Going through each one would require its piece, but here are a few more to consider:

The principle of action

It will happen more quickly if you perform the activity you wish to create. Sending entries to graduate schools for therapists, for instance, will begin things heading in the appropriate direction energetically if you intend to change occupations and get to be a therapist.

The law of relativity

We assign meaning and feelings to our experiences, but it's all relative in reality. There's always somebody suffering through things tougher than us, no matter how awful anything we're going through is.

If you want to study further manifestation, the principles of the universe might be a good place to start.

3. Energy Flows in the Direction of Your Concentration

According to Benson, one of the easiest ways to begin with manifestation is fantasizing. "We usually utilize our brains to worry or create a list of tasks we have to accomplish," she explains. Instead, she suggests you use your thoughts to be enthusiastic about life's prospects and to start envisioning what you may wish to do.

"Once you get up in the morning, make a general list of five things you'd want to do, whether they're urgent wishes or long-term aspirations," she suggests. "Before you go to bed, repeat the process. Start to dream higher than what you are today by using the ability of your imagination."

It is referred to as creative visualization by some practitioners. Aside from the mysticism, this technique makes sense. If you keep the things you intend to experience at the top of your mind at all times, you'll be more aware of opportunities to come closer to them when they arise.

4. You Aren't the Only One Who Matters

Practitioners need to be aware that manifestation isn't about ignoring what's happening in the world; it is usually condemned for being "optimistic frequency only" beliefs.

Yes, spreading optimism is a component of manifestation but it doesn't suggest we overlook hitches in our situations and the world. "We may recognize what we like to experience in our own lives and what we would want to find in the lives of others," Benson says. "Wishing for the better for the society and to others is a wonderful manifestation technique."

5. There Is No Fast Remedy

It's all too easy to terminate manifestation as a method of fast satisfaction. However, Benson believes expecting instant outcomes from a manifestation technique is like planting a tree and hoping it will grow strong and big overnight.

The Woke Mystix explains: "It requires compassion, confidence, and allowing for synchronization of intent and actualization to occur." It's equally important to consider the context of manifestation. "It's crucial to understand that we reside in an entrepreneurial system with perks and disadvantages while manifesting," they continue. For example, it might be difficult to materialize once you start with less due to cast, gender, education, color, etc. Manifestation may feel simpler if you have an advantage in certain areas. "Acknowledging our faults and advantages retains us fastened in the actual world though still consenting for the miracle of manifestation."

1.3 Important Elements

Manifestation is made up of three key elements. Each one is vital to the others, and they must be prioritized both individually and collectively.

1. Create it. It is where you may dream and visualize all of the wonderful things you desire in your life; then limit them down so you can pick which one to manifest.
2. Live it. Using the exercises, you may concentrate on being available in your life as now and convert negative thinking patterns into ones of thankfulness and joy.
3. Embrace it. Embracing and letting entails surrendering your mind and heart to the great rewards nature has in store for you... and guess what: You deserve everything!

1.4 Evolution of Manifestation

A lot of individuals are manifesting these days all over the world. The end product is quite remarkable. I opened my thoughts, made a prayer, and jotted down eight items I was prepared to receive only last month. These were lofty expectations that I didn't even consider realistic (due to limiting beliefs), yet within 24 hours, five of them had arrived at my door. All of them, plus more, in two weeks. Money, new friendships, and professional recognition are all things that come to mind.

Where did that strength originate from, anyway? How could I have been so blind to my sorcerous abilities? Why have I squandered so much time doubting myself?

These are questions that we may all ponder.

"Manifestation" was also a widespread notion in ancient Greece, with the primary distinction being that people couldn't perform it. Only Gods were allowed. When you consider how spirituality has evolved over millennia, it is intriguing. We're embracing creative power that was formerly solely designated for the gods when it relates to manifesting!

According to the Greeks, if a deity desired something to happen, it was almost guaranteed to happen unless it clashed with another deity. That is a significant contrast between now and back then. Gods were glorified with all of these human characteristics before then. Humans were continually attempting to figure out why they felt vindictive, lustful, delighted, or furious.

Today, we are at the mercy of our own mental and psychological obstacles rather than whimsical gods. It's all about alignment when engaging with our Greek godly superpowers. Here I'm preaching to myself. I've been considerably more prone to labor myself beyond exhaustion in the past. It's a long-standing family custom. It was a universal tradition, in fact: work exceedingly hard since the majority of life is already out of your control. But, all of a sudden, things have changed.

The internet has been saturated with new entities and free information during the last decade. Consequently, achieving our goals is more about altering our attention than chasing them.

More alignment with who we are and what we can contribute to the world means a lot less work for a greater reward. That was just not the case for the Old Greeks and even our forefathers and mothers. They lacked that type of adaptability. There weren't as many possibilities as there were before.

Because everything you desire is out there, you simply must prepare yourself to accept it. Alignment is more crucial than ever.

That's why I'd want to share a manifesting strategy that has done wonders for me in terms of aligning with what's truly achievable. Jennifer Blanchard, who is amazing, taught me this:

Fill in the blanks with the phrase "I'm open to receiving..." Refresh ten times and repeat. Stretch for a minimum of ten minutes! If it's only a matter of alignment getting in the way of your goals, intentionally expanding your mind enables magic to flow in.

1.5 Manifestation's Functionality

Successful manifestation must understand what we want, why

we desire it, and possibly why we haven't yet. It also necessitates self-assurance, faith in our objectives, a significant individual vibration, as well as a willingness to examine our deepest emotions. When we have these attributes, we can mute the voice in our thoughts that tells us we don't deserve or shouldn't have our life's desires. Then we start to shatter the negative thinking cycle we've been in for so long and establish new, more optimistic ones.

Chapter 2: PrincipleS and BenefitS of ManifeStation

Whether we are aware of it, we are continually creating our reality. Did you ever miss a train or bus because you were in a rush and worried about being late? Or has it ever happened to you that you desperately desired something but deep down didn't think it could be yours, and it never materialized?

These are all manifestation instances. The issue isn't knowing how to manifest; we all do it regularly. The real problem is figuring out how to manifest intentionally, so we don't feel weak and reliant on fate or other external sources.

I was pondering when I manifested anything that I didn't expect would happen in my life. These were minor miracles, and I realized right away that I had actively altered the path of events. You know how it feels when it's too late, things are looking horrible, and then everything turns out fine.

2.1 Principles   of   Manifestation

I've learned that we can alter any situation by making a deliberate decision. When we state unequivocally, "I need this no matter what" and "I chose it fully." It has a lot more power than you would think. It is purely coincidental that we are manifesting our preferred world. We ultimately receive what we want, and if we're exhausted from receiving what we don't want, it's time to become more mindful of unconscious manifestation. I want to present some principles that will help you achieve your goals. The only thing you have to do is stick with them.

Have a Clear Picture of What You Want to Achieve

You must be certain of your destination. It is the first step that cannot be avoided. It's like going on a journey without knowing where you're going. You can find yourself in your area, asking why you aren't in a more desirable location. You merely intended to be somewhere else without having a clear vision, and that's exactly what you got - you're somewhere else. You'll choose which plane to board once you know you're going to Hawaii. It's the case with anything else in your life. Your mind will connect your activities towards your objective once you have a direction.

Have a Great Desire to Succeed

Now that we know where we're heading, we need anything to help us get there. You're well aware that your plane will require gasoline to get there if you're going to Hawaii. The same is true for your vision; you'll need the correct fuel to make it a reality. Have a vision that motivates you and makes you feel lighter and happier every moment you think about it. These are the feelings that will lead you to your desired destination. Dare to dream large and think big; it will assist in energizing your vision.

Have a Clear Goal in Mind

It's all about intention in conscious manifestation. Assume that your vision will manifest at your command. Manifestation does not necessitate effort, but it necessitates concentrating on what you desire. Your desire will have clear instructions if you use intention. You instruct the energy where it may go by being focused. Imagine you want to open a yoga studio, but you spend all of your time on Instagram and texting with your friends. Although there is nothing intrinsically wrong with it, the fact remains that you lack the energy required to pursue your passion. To become a tangible reality, every dream requires a certain quantity of energy. It is when intention and focus come into play.

Develop Unflappable Beliefs

Most likely, you haven't manifested what you want since you don't believe it's possible. It is a very regular occurrence, and there is nothing wrong with it. However, if you don't believe you can have it, it won't happen. You are blocking the manifestation with your unbelief. Let's imagine you have a strong aim and a clear vision, but you don't believe it will happen for you. Then it's as if you say, "Actually, I can't have it." I don't think it can be mine." "So be it," says the universe. Why don't you think it can be yours? Investigate your beliefs to see what they are, and then change them.

Acceptance

Acceptance is the second fundamental of conscious manifestation. I don't intend to give up or have a 'whatever' attitude. I'm referring to your acceptance of the new idea and the fact that it is real for you and that you can get it. Accept the fact that it is already yours. Instead of focusing on why it won't work out, bow to your desires and embrace them in your life. Accept that it is what you need and also that you want it.

Take Coordinated Action

Align your behaviors with your desired outcome. If you want to tour the world, you'll either have to save more funds or have another means of income while you're on the trip. To anchor the energies, do what you'd do if you were confident it was already yours. In our scenario, by saving money for the trips, you're connecting yourself with the realization of your desire - you're demonstrating to the universe that you're positive you'll go by saving money.

Complete Dissociation

It is the point when the majority of individuals fail. We prefer to have control over things in our lives because we're worried that if we don't, they won't happen. And it is for this reason that we must let them go. If we're connected to something and insist on getting it RIGHT NOW, we're also implying that we don't believe we can have it. As a result, principle number four — forming an unshakeable belief — is jeopardized. You demonstrate that you believe it is truly yours by letting go of all when and how. Only those who are confident in the result may afford to wait.

Take Care of Yourself

Reality mirrors your strength back to you. If you think nature has forgotten about you and your aspirations, take a look at how you support them. By ignoring or retreating from your dreams, you create a world that ignores both you and your dreams.

Have the Clarity of a Laser Beam

A laser beam should be the "perfect" easy and intentional manifestation. With all of its force and purity, a laser beam is completely focused on one purpose. Just like the laser beam, we must be confident and focused. If something prevents you from believing in or concentrating on your objective, it will prevent you from realizing your ambition. I understand that being crystal clear and focused is challenging, but shorter periods may work wonders because, as I previously stated, the conscious decision can generate miracles. We may transform an undesirable consequence into something we desire if we determine our strength and effort.

Have Faith in the Process

Accepting your excellence right now, in this instant, is what leads to further greatness. Accepting that you're living in your intended manifestation is easier when you're in the situation. You live it when you feel it, regardless of what's happening around you. With enough time, the universe will catch up to your energy and your goals will manifest. The genuine process of co-creation is letting the manifestations follow your own belief.

Remember: the actual manifestation is feeling good—everything else is just frosting on the already wonderful cake!

Chill

The following phase in the manifestation process is critical. You must relax to properly manifest your wishes into reality. "Those who are assured of the outcomes may manage to wait and wait without concern," says A Course in Miracles.

Take that lesson with you and let it lead you to the conviction that you are on your path to getting what you want. Also, have faith that nature has a greater scheme than you do. Even if you know exactly what you desire, you have no control over when or how it will arrive.

Be Grateful

It is the last element, and I believe it is one that many people overlook. You feel so happy that you need to start again and manifest something different since you've acquired something so wonderful into your life without truly expressing gratitude to the cosmos. Spending five minutes each night and thinking about ten things you're grateful for from the previous day might drastically alter your outlook. I feel that writing about that particular day is quite beneficial because if you don't, you'll end up writing the same stuff repetitively. For me, yesterday's list included receiving a thank you text, having a coaching call that made me feel significantly lighter, having the opportunity to enjoy a new show on Television, having wonderful stuff in the fridge to prepare anything for dinner (fish finger sandwich, in case you were asking), and so on.

Take a moment to consider how lucky you are compared to others. You're doing better than the individual who lives in the stars if you're still alive.

2.2 Improvement in Life Through Manifestation

Imagine a method to reduce your tension, stress, and anxiety. I realize that seems like a hefty order. But let us investigate the possibility of finding a way to live more joyously and satisfyingly right now, within ourselves. This idea is the foundation of manifestation. Yes, manifesting "things" is exciting and joyful, but before we can manifest anything, we need to change our patterns of thinking, live fully in the present time, and be grateful for our lives as they are. You could be thinking right now that you took up this book to alter your life, not to continue living the life you've been living.

However, if you realize that life is very nice right now, at the present moment, you begin to recognize that life only happens in the current moment. It's where thankfulness may be found, and harnessing its power can change your life. Manifesting your heart's desire takes on new significance after you are excellent at truly experiencing your appreciation for the current moment.

Let's look at some of the walks of life where manifestations might be beneficial. (You'll pick up the techniques quickly.)

Professional Objectives

Perhaps you'd want to take on a managerial role at your workplace. You've put in a lot of effort in your current position and are confident that you'd make an excellent administrator. How might manifest assist you in achieving your goal? First, clearly understand what you need this job to comprise. Then, employing one or even more manifestation methods, such as journaling, believe and act as if it's already yours (in the imagination simply, of course). Following these stages will give you self-assurance, an admiration for where you are in your profession, and the capacity to anticipate and accept the position once it becomes open.

Relationships

Most individuals have undoubtedly thought about who their life partner is, what they appear like, what their nature is like, and what their lifestyle as a spouse may be like. Can you see this person becoming even more fantastic than you previously imagined if you've done this? Imagining and writing about your future spouse's physical characteristics, how they dress, how they communicate, and how the relationship progresses will help you identify and manifest what you truly desire in a life partner. You may manifest a deeper, more passionate partnership if you already have a partner. It's conceivable. The first step toward your heart's desire is defining it while believing with all your heart that it is on its way to you.

Finances

I could need some more cash. What are your thoughts? Over the years, I've noticed that some novices manifesting go immediately for the wealth and then abandon the concept when they don't get the jackpot the following day; it is depressing. Money manifesting is a little more difficult than manifesting other things because of the raw feelings that most of us have towards that, its scarcity, and availability. My recommendation is to start slowly, such as with a complimentary cup of coffee. Realizing that we can't have everything we desire right now is a part of this procedure. We need to put up the effort!

Fitness and Health

When you implement manifesting ideas to your fitness and health objectives, you'll discover that you're truly driven and excited to keep going on your fitness mission. It gets simpler to believe in the ability of your thoughts to make positive changes in this facet of life as you strive toward your fitness or health-related objectives and observe success. Since you may observe and experience the outcomes, the thrill becomes real. Please keep in mind that you need to continue to work with any healthcare providers you may have at this time.

2.3 Reasons for Failure in Manifestation

As you might be aware, most individuals cannot manifest anything and quit in loss or dissatisfaction. And who are they going to blame now since they haven't been able to materialize anything? Anybody but themselves.

Of course, they usually blame the entire notion of manifestation, claiming that "that there's no such phenomenon" or "the entire concept is crap"... or something along those lines. They deliberately overlook the truth that they were only a few days ago experimenting with the concept!

Why doesn't manifestation seem to deal with more people all of the time?

Your Manifestation Blocks Are Ignored

If your manifesting isn't succeeding, you may still face many obstacles. It would be best if you first resolved all key manifestation blockages to become completely connected with the universe (your subconscious imagination) and your desires and ambitions.

"Ask, Believe, Receive" is a well-known quotation from the movie and book The Secret.

To believe encompasses more than just your views or limiting ideas; I consider this section fairly comprehensive because it frequently takes some preparation to truly feel that you can attain your objectives and be receptive to receiving them.

I even take my hallmark manifesting technique a step further as, in my career as a coach, I've discovered that it's critical to remove your manifesting blockages before you establish your objectives (ask).

That's why I've reversed the script and advise you to address all significant abundance blockages before beginning the manifestation process. And it's for this reason that my manifestation method consistently produces results.

Limiting Beliefs

If you're puzzled why manifestation succeeds for some people but not for you, it's possible that you still need to focus on some major limiting beliefs.

As previously said, one of the manifesting blockages you need to overcome before beginning the process is limiting thoughts. Any fundamental limiting thoughts will keep you stuck and prevent you from progressing. You don't have to be ideal in your thoughts to be successful. You must, however, feel in a subliminal way that you are entitled to what you need. You must be self-assured and receptive to receive it. If you're trapped in a limiting pattern that you're acquainted with, you'll need to fix it before your energy can connect with what you want. Journaling and meditation are excellent self-reflection activities that may assist you in identifying your limiting beliefs and making the necessary attitude shift.

Attempting Against Someone's Will

If you're having trouble manifesting a certain person to do anything (like calling you or asking you out on a date), you may be overlooking the point of attraction. If you need the same things as someone else, you will attract that individual. But think about it. You transmit the vibration of lack if you attempt to manifest a certain individual against their choice. You wouldn't need to lure a specific individual if your thinking grew with plenty since there would be enough possibilities suitable for you. Instead of focusing all of your attention on a single individual, concentrate on the emotions and characteristics you want to manifest. You could discover that the person you're attempting to attract was never the correct fit for you in the first place, and you're instead attracting someone much better for you.

Improper Goal Setting

You may have been begging the Holy Spirit for the stuff you want. Typically, it takes the form of objectives. However, just putting down your objectives on a piece of paper and then forgetting about them will not get you very far. You must establish the correct kinds of objectives for your manifestation to function. Three sorts of objectives will assist you in realizing your dreams. There are three types of goals: breakthrough, result, and process.

Breakthrough objectives are significant. They're motivating and will get you out of bed every morning. They must be so intriguing and appealing that you look forward to going to work every day. Breakthrough goals are intended to help you build a dramatically improved life for yourself, and they should be established to motivate and inspire you. The outcome objectives are a bit more explicit. An outcome goal can be something like: "I want to be in the right position spiritually, emotionally, and physically by the same day next year, and I'll be the ideal match for my dream person," where a breakthrough objective would be something vague and lofty. They are more concrete and provide you with a working timeframe. The daily action tasks you will take are known as process goals. What behaviors will you adopt daily to help you become the ideal companion for anyone? Process goals will resemble a regular to-do list to track your progress and accomplishments. If you set these kinds of objectives for yourself, you'll have a far higher chance of getting all you desire.

Being Impatient

Are you attempting to make things happen in your life through force?

Remember that whatever frequency you're resonating at is the frequency you'll attract. If you're impatient, it means you require something. When you require anything, you are in a state of scarcity. Get out of the rut of scarcity and put your faith in the process. The universe likes to move fast and with minimal opposition. Allow the naturally joyful energy flow to come to you as you get over the impatience's temporal limits. When speed comes naturally, it happens. When it's forced, it doesn't happen. Still, I understand if your manifestations make you frustrated.

Taking No Action

Another reason the Law of Attraction isn't working for you is that you're concentrating too much on believing rather than doing. We've been taught that you'll get it if you believe in something. At least, that's what books such as The Secret tell us, don't they? It is especially true if you're working toward a goal.

Taking action is the same as receiving. You must believe, take action, and create an effort to reach your objectives when generating ideas. The first step in changing your vibration is to believe in yourself. However, if you begin to make an effort, you will be on your way to accomplishing your goals.

Inappropriate Tools Usage

When used appropriately, manifestation techniques may be quite effective. Keep in mind that the correct instrument for one person may not be appropriate for another. Visualization may be preferable to affirmations for certain people. Both may be beneficial to someone else. The essential thing is to experiment with various law of attraction techniques to see which ones trigger your energy to shift.

You must discover the proper tools for you among affirmations, meditation, visualization, hypnosis, NLP, and ERP. When you find it, you'll begin to feel the way you want to feel, and your inner life will begin to change, causing exterior change.

Improper Implementation of Manifestation Steps

They will work if you execute the manifestation procedures exactly. If you approach them incorrectly, you may find yourself in some difficulty. You won't use the Law of Attraction if you just read about it. To alter your subconscious mind, you must first change your conscious mind, focus on your manifestation blockages (one by one), set the correct goals, and take driven action. Using the Law of Attraction would be a work in progress.

You may discover details you might have not understood previously as you continue studying and working with it.

2.4 Time Taken by 369 Method to Work

The Law of Attraction is aided by the 369 manifestations, a structured programming approach. But what is it precisely, and how long would it need for the manifestation to occur?

The 369 Manifestation approach should take 45 days on average to function, but you must be persistent. When writing your mantra and manifesting objectives, remember to follow the 17-second guideline: 3 times when you first wake up, 6 times during the day, and 9 times before bedtime.

Nikola Tesla, a well-known scientist, thought that the digits 3,6, and 9 have a deep cosmic significance. He learned that if we can grasp the significance of this numerical pattern, we may tap into its power. These figures may be utilized to create the ideal manifestation method and scripting practice. However, the cosmos needs time to function. As a result, why does your manifestation take 45 days to occur when you use the 369 manifestation technique?

It is because the Law of Attraction takes time to function. You must clearly define what you want and jot it down regularly. Your desires are imprinted on your subconscious mind as a result of this. When your subconscious mind understands your objectives, your vibrational energy shifts. Then you start to fulfill the desire you're looking for, and attraction occurs.

The 369 manifestation writing concentrates on your objective and instills passion, faith, and confidence in your ability to create it.

The Law of Attraction will not function if you do not think your desires will be fulfilled. It is possible to manifest your wish in 6 weeks by scripting many times each day.

Many people, however, have had their manifestations far sooner than 45 days. Some people have been able to link with their wants rapidly, and attraction has developed within days. However, I've seen that some people's manifestations take months or even years to arrive, and I've also seen that other individuals never acquire their manifestations. Although recommending a strategy is effective, no one can ensure its achievement.

Chapter 3: TechniqueS and Method of ManifeStation

Let's get started, shall we? I enjoy discussing all of the numerous techniques and methods for manifesting. There is much more we may do daily to pull ourselves up to a level of delight. Educating ourselves on how to remain in that position of joy, appreciation, and contentment is the key to these strategies. It is where these tools come into play. Learning to be artistic and have fun with your thoughts may help maintain your mind in a happy and positive state of mind. Being in that state of happiness raises your vibration, enabling you to lure everything you seek into your life.

3.1 Techniques of Manifestation

Remember that, according to the Law of Attraction, like attracts like. Therefore, staying "upbeat and cheerful" draws "upbeat and joyful." As you advance in adjusting your thinking patterns, using some or all of the preceding tactics numerous times a day, together with journaling, will remind you to be optimistic, focused, and cheerful. You may discover that you prefer certain tactics over others when you try them out. Don't be too hard on yourself, but give them all a go first. If you decide later that you want to modify something, knowing all the options will be useful.

Visualization

Did you ever fantasize about being younger and what you'd do with your life when you were old? The majority of us did. And that's exactly what you have to do here: "daydream." Allow yourself sufficient time to sit quietly and imagine, letting your mind run wild. Do you want to take a ride on an elephant? Why not, right? Do you want to go to the furthest reaches of the universe? Make it happen! What you can achieve with your imagination knows no bounds! It may sound foolish at first to use this visualization approach, but the more you allow yourself to pretend like you did once you were a kid, the more real and substantial your thoughts become. Visualizing daily may liberate your imagination to explore infinite possibilities!

Vision Board

A vision board, also known as a dream board, is an attractive display that you may regularly look at and let sink into your conscious. A vision board is a physical space where you may utilize graphical representations of your mental images to build a tool to help you stay focused. A posters board is an excellent choice for creating a vision board. Your vision board would be quite personal, and it should be displayed in a prominent area where you can read it frequently. To make a vision board, clip or glue photographs (and text, if desired) from websites and social media and drawings you've made to exhibit all of your ambitions and wishes in one spot. Words and photographs of items, people, activities, and graphics that express emotions may be included on your board. It may include whatever you like, and you can update it or create a new one at any time.

Meditation

As an instructor in the subject, I may go on and on about the advantages of meditation, but for the sake of manifestation, sitting in quiet every day is necessary to begin to change how you view your life, yourself, and the world. Establishing a meditation practice helps you set aside some time each day (even if it's only 10 minutes) to be still. There will be "must-do" ideas when meditating at times. Gently toss them to the back and sit, allowing yourself to simply be. It's a good idea to keep in mind that you don't have to sit in a specific posture with your folded arms correctly; sit wherever you're most comfortable. It doesn't matter how you do it as far as you're doing it right.

Affirmations

Louise Hay, a motivational speaker, promoted the technique of chanting positive affirmations to oneself in the 1970s. Today, this technique is commonly utilized to boost self-esteem, confidence, and self-love. Simply saying "I love you" while staring in the mirror is a powerful affirmation, to begin with. It might be disconcerting and difficult to do it for the first time. However, if you repeat this sentence to yourself multiple times each day, you will notice that it has a beneficial effect on your self-esteem. Finding or writing positive mantras to repeat throughout the day may become fun and powerful creative activity.

Scripting and Journaling

Journaling and scripting are hands-on strategies for manifesting, similar to visualization, in which you fantasize without constraints. When you journal, you convey your wishes to the universe and your optimistic ideas about receiving them. Scripting is the technique of writing situations where you previously have what you're trying to generate. For example, if you want to visit a certain place, you should write about the views, sounds, scents, and other sensations as if you've already had them. Scripting regularly allows you to experience what it would be like to achieve your goals.

Focus Wheel

The concentration wheel is an easy yet powerful manifestation tool for shifting your focus from restricting to refreshing ideas. It's simple to make one: Start by making a little circle on a piece of paper or a board and writing down the aim or dream you want to attain right now. Then, throughout the circle, scribble down positive thoughts linked to your main goal.

If your objective is to improve your health, for example, positive phrases may include "I will work out five days a week" and "I will eat healthy food, be more attentive to cuisine." This manifestation technique aids in the visualization of your thoughts.

Act "as if"

Adopting Alfred Adler's behaving "as if" approach may be a speedier way to acquire what you want in your life. Acting as if you've already accomplished what you want, rather than waiting for it to happen, is a manifestation approach that argues for lasting behavioral adjustments that might put you on the rapid track to achieving whatever it is you're seeking to manifest. Rather than continually speculating and planning for a future occurrence, this strategy pushes you to take action right now and act as if you have what you're manifesting.

55x5 and 3-6-9 Methods

The 555, a powerful and relatively recent manifestation technique, is 55X5. Create a line or two describing your wishes/ ambitions as if it's already been achieved, and write it 55 times per day for 5 days to employ this approach. The 3-6-9 approach requires you to write your wish three times in the morning, six times in the noon, and nine times at night for 45 days. To keep your energy high, it's crucial to be as specific as possible while articulating your objective and be positive when writing.

Bottom Line

Whether you want to manifest love, success, or happiness, manifestation methods may be quite effective in attaining your goals. Although there is minimal scientific evidence to support those strategies based on the Law of Attraction concept, so far research shows they can surely assist you in accomplishing your goals.

Investigate these manifesting methods to find which ones work best for you — You can practice some or all at once, or you can alter or mix them to create a version that suits your needs.

3.2 Method of Manifestation

You're aware that manifesting works for others, but you're unsure what you're lacking to make it work for you. The most common reason individuals become confused while manifesting is that they are unaware of the necessary steps to manifest and co-create with the universe. Doesn't it sound fantastic? But how precisely are you expected to manifest something? Here are some steps to manifesting whatever you wish.

1. Define your objectives

The initial step is to set a goal. Choose your goals, whether you desire to find true love, change employment, improve your health, or succeed in a different hobby.

Consider the following:

- Is there anything you've always wanted to accomplish but haven't got the chance to do?
- At this point in your life, what will you most prefer out of anything in the world?

2. Be specific about your requirements

The next stage is to seek what you wish in the real world. Some people like to make vision boards, write about their goals in notebooks, pray, or talk about their goals with dear ones or mentors. The most important thing is to be clear about your objectives and to be able to see how your life would improve as a result.

Questions to ponder:

- What would it be like?
- How could my life change if I accomplished my objective?
- How would it appear?

3. Make a strategy for moving forward

While your thoughts and mindset are important in manifesting, examining the precise behaviors required to reach your goal is equally important. Even the loftiest goal may be broken down into small chunks. If you wish to change jobs, the first step can be to research a new field or find someone who has worked in it.

Question to ponder:

- What should my first little step toward obtaining this goal be?
- Do you have any suggestions for new skills I should learn?
- Do I have access to any specialists?

4. Change your attitude

Now arrives the most important part: practicing mindfulness. You must focus on positivity and gratitude as you work toward your goals. Are you familiar with the "Law of Attraction"? You would like to put out positive energy to receive positive energy back. It takes some thought about your mental patterns. If you're convincing yourself because you're not competent enough, it's time to go deeper and figure out why you have these beliefs - and change them with new, healthier ones. Consider it like getting into your emotional wheel: you want to steer it in the path of your goals.

Question to ponder:

- What changes do I need to make to fully believe I deserve what I desire?
- How can I align my ideas and self-beliefs with my objectives?

5. Keep an open mind

When an opportunity arises, you may say to yourself, "What if?" "That's it! It's exactly what I was searching for!" — yet it sneaks up on you. Visualizing an objective may take time, even when working and having the right mindset. Have trust that it will all work out when the right opportunity arises. Also, keep your eyes open since the "perfect opportunity" might not always present itself in the way you think!

3.3 Practice Consistently

Now that you've mastered some of the most common manifestation strategies, it's time to bring them all together, be creative, and realize that consistency is the key to success.

The tone for the entire process is set by generating a very clear intention of what you're manifesting. The more specific your goal is, the easier it will be to envision, allowing it to manifest more quickly.

Start the practice of paying attention and recognizing your negative vs good thoughts and feelings throughout the day once you've established your goal.

This procedure is a critical component of the entire series. Recognize negative ideas and feelings as soon as they arise and rephrase them positively. Affirmations, meditation, vision boards, and other strategies can help. You may expel negativity from your being and bring in happiness, pleasure, and joy by staring at your vision board, journaling in your diary, scripting, meditating, and utilizing positive affirmations several times a day.

Changing your negative thinking processes to positive ones, on the other hand, requires you to accept the result. You must believe and fully understand that you deserve everything good that life has to offer! Commit to consistency going in, set the intents and strategies in place, then set aside time every day, throughout the day, to do the job with this conviction in your mind.

3.4 Reasons to Be Consistent in Manifestation

You'll have terrific days during this manifestation process when you feel like you've conquered the bad habits that are preventing you from manifesting anything and changed them into very positive, high-vibrational routines. Prepare yourself, though: there will be days when you seem dejected and as if the

universe is working against you! Fear not, and keep in mind the following:

- Developing the transformation of muscle takes time. To achieve results, you must maintain your training program, just like exercising.

- On days when you're feeling down, you need to be kind to yourself. The most important point to keep in mind is to keep going... never stop. On good days, visualization, affirmations, writing, and thankfulness are simple, but the real work begins on bad days.

- If you're having a bad day, pushing yourself to create a list of what you're grateful for will help you feel better. "When in dispute, drop and give me five grateful," is my mantra. It is to say, at the absolute least, be grateful daily.

- If you're having more bad days than good days, it's time to reassess your manifesting strategy. Consider analyzing the skills you use daily and altering the time you spend performing them or focusing on the ones you enjoy more than others. Aside from consistency, there is no one-size-fits-all approach to any of this. It's all up to you to figure out what works best for you.

3.5 Let's Get Started

Getting organized might assist you in maintaining the consistency required for overall manifesting success. You can focus more on the steps if you plan for the week. With step 1: Create It, you've probably already considered what you'd like to create as a first option. Now is the time to focus on the specifics of what you want. Consider how you feel about the item you want and how it appears. Consider how different your life would be if

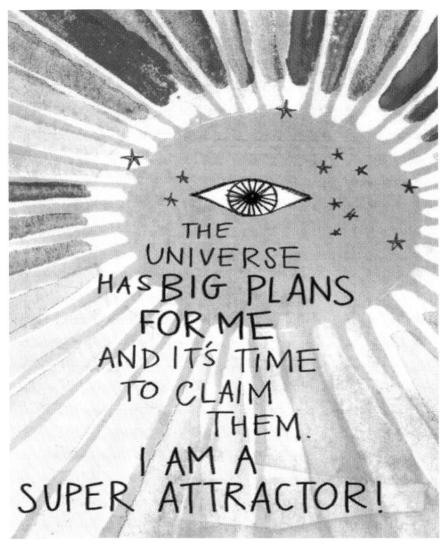

you had it. Make sure you understand exactly what "it" is. Step 2 is about planning and spreading out the approaches you'll use so you may accomplish the task numerous times during the day.

Here are a few suggestions to get you started: Perhaps you start each day by expressing thanks and meditating. Then you focus on affirmations till mid-morning. You write in your journal during your lunch break. If you're using the 55x5 or 3-6-9 approach, follow the instructions to incorporate the strategy into your day. Perhaps you focus on the vision board or sit and picture your life in the evening. Then, as the evening progresses, you work on scripts and continue to write in your notebook about what you're grateful for. Whatever daily practice you choose, thank the universe every night while you go to bed for all the wonderful things that are coming your way. It is the third step: Accept it. Never lose sight of the fact that this step is equally as crucial as the first two.

Bottom Line

Manifesting is a goal-setting technique that stresses the significance of being present in the moment. Your ideas shape your world. Negative self-talk and a fixation on difficulties might stymie your growth. When you attempt to reframe negative beliefs, you will feel more secure and optimistic about your future achievement. All of that optimism and self-assurance may assist you in attracting the possibilities you desire.

Chapter 4: BaSicS of the LaW of Attraction

The Law of Attraction is undoubtedly the most well-known 12 universal principles. Simply expressed, this spiritual concept states that like attracts like, and that good thought may bring about a more positive reality. "Notice your thoughts, they become your words; observe your words, they became your actions; notice your actions, they develop your habits; observe your habits, they create your character; observe your character, it's becoming your destiny," stated Lao Tzu, a traditional Chinese philosopher.

The concept of attracting what we project has existed from ancient eras, and many people credit Buddha as the first to introduce it to the world. The points between manifestation and attraction's law are connected in this chapter. You'll discover the relationship between these ideas and how they're influenced by our emotional states and the critical role gratitude plays in manifesting the life we want. You'll also discover the value of focusing attention on your thoughts and how to use the power of your mind to halt bad habits in their tracks. Opening up to new views and ideologies brings up a whole new world of possibilities.

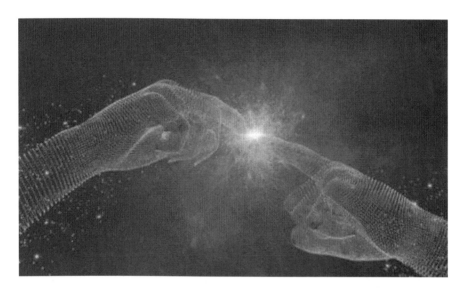

4.1 Definition of Law of Attraction

The Law of Attraction theory is grounded on the modest principle of "like entices like." It means that any energy we send out into the environment will attract similar events and individuals to us. It is up to us whether the energy is pleasant or unpleasant. Here's an example of "like attracts like" in action: When you meet someone, you immediately sense a connection with them. You could have surprisingly similar thoughts and lifestyles and the same sense of humor. Whether it's friendship or not, you sense a spark of desire. Everything on our globe (and beyond) is made out of energy and vibrates continually. To summarize the Law of Attraction, everyone attracts what they put out through their energies and vibration.

On the other hand, most of humanity never understands universal rules like the Law of Attraction or prefers not to believe in them. However, there is some good news: Regardless of your beliefs, you're always operating as a human magnet, giving and receiving the same vibrational frequency from the cosmos. It's impossible to avoid using the Law of Attraction. It's something you do all the time. The Law of Attraction is constantly in action. It makes no difference whether you believe in it or not. Saying you don't trust in the laws of attraction is the same as saying you don't believe in gravity. Whether you accept it or not, the cosmos is unconcerned.

Of course, you may choose not to believe it and work your tail off for the rest of your life, wondering why you aren't getting what you want. But I'm here to encourage you that you don't have to work 80 hours a week to live a fulfilling life. I'm here to inspire you to think that you can live a happy, carefree life while still attaining your goals. Have you ever thought of a buddy you haven't spoken to in a while and then received a call from them later that day? Isn't it crazy?

The majority of individuals dismiss such events as coincidences. It's not the case. It's a matter of the Law of Attraction. So, why isn't everyone utilizing this tool if it works? Because the vast majority of people get it wrong.

When most individuals conceive of the Law of Attraction, they believe the following: "If I think about a million dollars for a long time and hard enough, the universe will send it to me." So, what's this? It's not the case. Here's how it appears in real life:

If you genuinely want to be a billionaire, feel you deserve it, and get your ass up and do the job, the universe will help you figure out how to make it happen.

4.2 Mechanism of the Law of Attraction

According to the law of vibration, everything in the world is moving or vibrating with energy. This rule states that the apple we're eating is energy, as are the big trees outside and the automobile we're driving. Furthermore, we are made out of energy, always moving and vibrating. Every object we touch, see, and think about, including ourselves, vibrates at different frequencies. Since like attracts like, we draw peace and calm into our life when we vibrate calm and peace via our thoughts and deeds.

Similarly, vibrating pleasantly attracts happy people and circumstances into our lives. If we continuously radiate negativity via our thoughts and behaviors, we will attract bad things or people into our lives. According to Concha, everything in your current life, from your house and relationship to your job, results from your thinking. "You will see a link between your ideas and what you have in your reality if you pay attention." Manifesting is another term for this, she clarifies. "Everything you encounter is drawn to you since the LOA is reacting to the beliefs you expressed at some point."

The concept is simple: when you concentrate on something or someone, you produce a vibratory link that pulls them to you. "It entails being aware of my thoughts rather than responding to them. The idea you're focused on in the present now has created a vibration within you, and the LOA is responding to it right now, whether you recall a previous occurrence, witness something in the present, or picture something in the future," she explains.

4.3 History of the Law of Attraction

Whether you're a novice to the Law of Attraction or have been practicing manifestation for some time, you may have pondered where the essential concepts originated. Is it a somewhat recent occurrence? Is it a result of old teachings? Has it always been described in the same manner?

Have we gotten better at harnessing our manifestation potential? These details are frequently overlooked in Law of Attraction books and publications. Learning them, on the other hand, can greatly improve your comprehension.

We'll look at the origins of manifestation in this piece of the true history of the Law of Attraction. We may also track how our understanding of the Law of Attraction's meaning and science has evolved throughout time.

We'll consider the contributions of important authors on the subject throughout. We'll also provide some educated guesses on where the manifestation field could be heading in the future.

If we go far enough back in time; we may find the origins of the Law of Attraction in various ancient traditions and Eastern philosophies. While it wasn't known as the Law of Attraction in the classical era, it was mentioned in Buddhist and Christian texts.

The Buddha, for instance, popularly stated that our ideas shape who we are. Furthermore, Jesus' words might be understood as a message about our boundless ability to create.

Since the Law of Attraction has constantly influenced the direction of our life, it is usually assumed that humanity has always been aware of it (even if only subconsciously). However, it wasn't until Madame Helena Blavatsky's work that the phrase "Law of Attraction" was coined.

The emergence of the New Vision phenomenon may be traced back to the nineteenth century. As a result, notions like manifestation made their way into popular awareness. While many authors contributed to this vital growth phase, Helena Blavatsky and Thomas Troward became two of the most prominent ones.

Blavatsky, Helena Petrovna

In the nineteenth century, Helena Blavatsky provided spiritual advice and teaching worldwide. She had a character for being spiritually talented at this point. In her book The Secret Doctrine, she relied on old religious traditions. Much of what she thought was similar to what we today refer to as "The Law of Attraction."

She said, particularly, that our perceptions of ourselves or our identities characterize who we are and what we're capable of. She stressed our potential to change reality and our ability to transcend our constraints.

Both of these lessons may be found in manifestation teachings today.

Similarly, several of the most important modern Law of Attraction books, like The Secret, is widely thought to have been influenced by Thomas Troward's studies in the 19th century. Some have labeled him a "mystic Christian." He also agreed with Madame Blavatsky that the best way to learn is to combine ideas from other spiritual traditions.

In the Early Twentieth Century

Law of Attraction research exploded in the early twentieth century with pioneering and inspirational writings from Helena Blavatsky and Thomas Troward. A diverse group of authors contributed their viewpoints on the topic of manifestation. Many of them use personal instances of accomplishment to emphasize their views. As we look at the writings of a handful of the most well-known and intriguing early twentieth-century practitioners, we'll note that many of them coined terminology and theories that we now use when dealing with the Law of Attraction.

William Walker Atkinson, 1906

Law of Attraction practitioners may work on increasing their willpower, sharpening their attention, and building magnetism that draws wonderful things into their life, as William Walker Atkinson explains.

He wrote almost 100 novels during his lifetime. He practiced law besides his writing for a while. Later in life, he returned to the field of law. He was a co-editor of a famous New Thought journal and a related magazine. His goal was to raise awareness of manifestation and urge people to build on his concepts. Much of his most respected colleagues were practicing Hindus, and his Law of Attraction research incorporated important elements from Hindi spiritual beliefs. Some of the vocabulary and intellectual frameworks he gave in his teachings, such as notions about raising vibration, are still in use today.

1910, The Science of Becoming Rich, Wattles

Wallace Delois Wattles, wrote the book The Science of Becoming Rich (issued in 1910), sparking a fresh awareness of the Law of Attraction. Modern audiences are still reading his works. Among some of the primary lessons of The Science of Becoming Rich is cultivating our manifestation capacity rather than relying on others to teach us.

Wattles, who enjoyed collaborating with various New Thought workers, frequently gave seminars in addition to releasing his books. In this way, he could propagate his teachings far and wide. He provided simple, easy-to-understand procedures that everyone may utilize. He highlighted that we might apply these principles to our drive for wealth. He also promoted creative imagery, which is still a big part of the Law of Attraction today.

1937 – Think and Grow Rich by Napoleon Hill

Napoleon Hill started his professional life as a reporter. However, he became renowned after publishing Think and Grow Rich in 1937, which detailed his Law of Attraction ideas. He sought to explain how we may overcome our issues and employ manifestation techniques to create a joyful, successful life by leaning on his personal experiences.

He was not as affected by religious instructors as other Law of Attraction writers, such as Ralph Waldo Emerson. Our knowledge of how negative thinking ideas draw more toxicity into our life is largely due to Napoleon Hill. Most modern Law of Attraction trainees agree with his assertion that trusting in our potential increases that potential. He also urged people to determine their life's purpose and strive toward it.

In the Mid-to-Late Twentieth Century

In the mid-to late-twentieth century, the Law of Attraction only grew in popularity and influence. Jerry and Esther Hicks, for example, came to popularity in the 1980s by claiming to be able to channel communications from non-physical creatures. The Teachings of Abraham, a collection of nine books by Esther Hicks, explains how the Law of Attraction occurs in a very approachable way. It also includes advice on applying the Law of Attraction to manifest the objects you want.

Meanwhile, Louise Hay, a New Thought author, has played a key role in popularizing the notion of employing affirmations to help you achieve your Law of Attraction aspirations. She also assisted Law of Attraction practitioners to recognize the potential of a positive self-concept to enhance the vibration and improve your capacity to manifest as a supporter of self-love and self-compassion.

Richard Weiss and W. Clement Stone are two more important Law of Attraction authors from the mid-to-late twentieth century. Clement Stone and Napoleon Hill collaborated on a book on attracting success.

Meanwhile, Weiss is notable for linking the Law of Attraction to the idea of non-resistance, which he coined. According to this theory, we attract objects when we deliberately put energy into resisting them.

The Secret and the History of the 21st Century Law of Attraction

Rhonda Bryne's book The Secret (and its accompanying film) has elevated the Law of Attraction from a fringe notion to a global phenomenon in the twenty-first century. The Secret provides the perspectives and teachings of a diverse group of well-known and up-and-coming Law of Attraction experts. Jack Canfield, Joe Vitale, and Marie Diamond all contributed insight to the film. The movie is noted for its direct, inspiring approach to manifesting. For example, it emphasizes creating objectives, pondering on negativity, and developing innovative thinking to achieve what you truly desire. Viewers and readers leave his material feeling that anybody can benefit from the Law of Attraction, that it is not limited to professionals or the spiritually advanced.

Both the movie and the book were huge hits. The secret taught us that we all can create our world and that "thoughts can become things," as Bryne frequently says. The book managed to sell more than 20 million copies and has a large celebrity following.

Will Smith, for instance, attributes most of his great experiences to the practice of the Law of Attraction. Oprah Winfrey has also pushed The Secret to the audience. Boxer Conor McGregor, meanwhile, has stated that he "dared to dream his victory into reality."

Chapter 5: PrincipleS, Application, and BenefitS of the LaW of Attraction

This chapter will discuss the principles of the Law of Attraction as well as its pros and cons. We can achieve our goals in some specific areas of life through the Law of Attraction, which will be discussed in this chapter.

5.1 Principles of the Law of Attraction

There are several different perspectives on the Law of Attraction, how it functions, and whether it appears to work. But, in the end, it all boils down to one simple concept: "like attracts like." I will build everything I desire in my life if I honestly think I can. Miracles will happen if I expect them to. If, on the other hand, that horrible, nasty voice in my brain convinces me that I'm not strong enough to have my innermost ambitions come true—and I believe it—I'll never get what I want. As a result, the actual secret to manifesting virtually whatever you genuinely desire is to employ all of the tools available to you to increase your vibration and fight negative ideas and attitudes. Tragically, some people never seem to break free from their negative mental patterns. However, if you yield to the manifestation process and put in the effort, your life will change in such a manner that you'll be amazed at how far you've gone when you look back! The following principles can assist you in your quest.

Change Your Attitude

You might be asking how to avoid thinking negative beliefs at this point. It is when things start to get exciting. When you start paying attention to your thoughts, you'll notice your thinking patterns emerge. Please keep track of when you have negative thoughts and what causes them. Setting aside a few days to make a concentrated effort to notice your thoughts is a smart idea. Once you've identified your triggers, you may use affirmations, keywords, or phrases to quickly pull yourself out of that gloomy area and into a more optimistic mindset.

Avoid Negative Beliefs

Due to the negative views you hold, you might be well conscious that you have harsh thoughts about particular events and individuals (maybe even yourself). Are you eager to let go of your negative thoughts and take a fresh look at those persons and situations? Simply altering your perspective to compassion may profoundly influence your inner self. Rather than hiding out once you run into that annoying classmate on the street, remember to yourself, "I am love," and welcome them. Keep an eye on what occurs next. It's amazing what a little kindness for yourself and others may do.

Make Space for Positive Thoughts

Deciding to be more optimistic has power. Identifying when your attention wanders and replacing it with something cheerful or love-centered can help you achieve a profound mindset transformation. For instance, instead of obsessing on the bad aspects of being alone and blaming them for not following through, thank the Lord that you didn't hook up with them and understand that you now have space for your ideal companion to come up! In this sense, shifting your viewpoint from pessimism to optimism is crucial to altering your ideas.

Prepare a List of Specific Goals and Objectives

What are you hoping to achieve in life? You should refine your aspirations and establish objectives for yourself while changing your mentality to one of positivity and thankfulness. These objectives should be focused on changing your mindset and identifying what you intend to achieve. Performing all of these activities simultaneously and having the intents and concept transfers at the back of the mind are critical to the process's effectiveness.

The More Specific, the Better

Once you've identified what you desire, ask yourself, "Why do I need this specific thing?" as you refine your wishes to the universe. You inquire as to why and evaluate the response. You will discover your truth by repeating this process and searching deep. This practice will assist you in gaining awareness in your mind and keeping your attention on your actual desires.

5.2 The Benefits of Applying the Law of Attraction

As Concha says, things may begin to alter for the best if you begin employing the LOA.

Lucky Person

Concha claims that while you can't be particular about the goods or people you materialize with LOA, you may improve your chances of acquiring them. She continues, "You may manifest events, chances, relationships, and objects." "Can you recall a moment when you desired something or imagined a circumstance, and it came true? Some may refer to it as 'luck,' but it is merely the LOA in action."

Assist You to Gain Your Ground

Are you in need of a total mental makeover? The LOA, as Concha explains, might be exactly that. "Your entire view will alter once you grasp how the LOA works," she explains. "You understand that you have the power to lead the life you deserve; you don't need to compromise. You may manifest your desired future with ease and fluidity. You'll become more aware of yourself and more anchored. It's going to be a game-changer."

Spiritual Repercussions

Since it digs into people's devoutness, the Law of Attraction may produce results. Devoutness has been related to several health rewards, such as less anxiety, improved strength, reduced depression, and improved overall well-being. Many individuals feel that the perception is operative as it is linked with God or the universe with our wishes. This viewpoint proposes that we all are created with energy that works at different frequencies. Consequently, it's essential to change adverse thoughts with good ones, chiefly thankfulness for what we presently have.

We may shift the frequency of our power by employing thankful, positive thoughts and sentiments and concentrating on our aspirations instead of our difficulties, so the Law of Attraction will bring wonderful things into our life. What we attract is determined by where and how we direct our focus, but we must feel that it is now ours or soon.

Enhanced Happiness

Employing the Law of Attraction could also positively influence one's mental fitness. We generally take more chances, observe more possibilities, and bring new options when we concentrate on attaining a new authenticity and trusting it is attainable. Once we don't believe anything is probable for us, on the other side, we prefer to allow openings to cross us overlooked. We act in ways that damage our pleasure prospects when we feel we don't deserve nice things. We might reverse bad outlines in our lives and swap them with more positive, beneficial, and effective ones by altering our self-talk and attitudes regarding life. A good event can attract others, and a life's path may alter from a descending curved to upward scaling. Improving self-talk may transform your life in a good way, which is one of the bases of many forms of therapy. Cognitive-behavioral therapy (CBT), a widely used and successful treatment for various disorders, is based on recognizing and modifying habitual negative beliefs.

This generates optimistic outcomes and helps people achieve better mental fitness.

5.3 Disadvantages of Using the Law of Attraction

Before you run out to get your diary and get going, you should be aware of a few points since the LOA is not without its drawbacks. Before you attempt anything, make sure to follow these experts' advice.

You May Attract Negativity

So, you're fixated on someone who you know is poisonous. As per the LOA, that might be a risky game to play. You could be drawing someone into your life if you're allowing anyone to live rent-free in the imagination. "You have to make sure you're mindful of your ideas," Concha advises. "What you're contemplating about isn't judged by the LOA. You will draw anything you pay attention to into your life, whether it is 'good' or 'bad.' Consider yourself a magnet that attracts the soul of your thoughts and feelings."

It Is Not Magic

Do you need to get a million dollars? We've got some awful news for you. The LOA is not a mystical power that will perform your bidding, unlike what you might have heard. "You can't attract health if you're feeling sick," Concha explains. "You can't attract success if you're poor because it's against the law."

5.4 The Law of Attraction and Its Applications

The Law of Attraction may be used to achieve various objectives mentioned in the following.

Relationships and Love

The first step in applying the Law of Attraction to lure more fondness into your life is recognizing how you could subconsciously oppose it.

"If the universe keeps delivering you unavailable individuals," Kaiser explains, "this might signal anything within you remains inaccessible." Once you've identified the obstacle, you can focus on tearing down these inner walls and developing a more open relationship approach. Trust nature to deliver you the relationship you want, not exactly the one you believe you want, by tuning in to who you are and what you desire.

Career Goals

It's critical to be explicit about what you want while using the Law of Attraction in your job career.

Make clear statements about your job ambitions, such as "I would like to work with like-minded individuals who support my views" or "I earn X amount of dollars in X place." And, of course, an effort is essential. If you desire that promotion, think about what the 'promoted-me' would do.

Finances

Financial anxieties are real and understandable, and it takes a great deal of unlearning to have a successful relationship with wealth.

It's particularly easy to get into a limited point of view regarding money. Rather than focusing on what you don't have, try to concentrate on what you do have. "Abundance pours from me so I may cheerfully share," Kaiser says in one of his mantras.

It's advisable to start small in all of the domains mentioned above and focus on making tiny adjustments first. The more you practice, the more effective you'll get at manifesting until you're ready to handle greater, more life-altering changes.

The bottom line: While the Law of Attraction may appear too wonderful to be true—and it might take some practice to master— at its foundation, it's about transforming your perspective to one of luxury, bringing in whatever you want, and connecting your actions with your aspirations. You may become the creator of your life and attract many opportunities to achieve those elements.

5.5 Step by Step Method of the Law of Attraction

Manifestation experts are people who can elevate their vibration and maintain it for long periods. Of course, you can't always be happy and upbeat, but that's not what you seek anyhow. It's simply a matter of letting go of unneeded negativity and bad vibrations and concentrating instead on the lifestyle you would like to live.

Our prevailing emotions and ideas underpin the entire manifestation process. As a result, manifestation is triggered by our better ideas and, more crucially, the feelings that accompany these beliefs. As a result, we wish to pay attention to these sentiments daily.

Here are some measures you may take to boost your vibration, enhance the energy, and lure the greatness you've ever wanted:

Get Into a State of Steady Positive Frequency

Being optimistic does not mean avoiding the negative at all

costs. Our lives are constantly in balance: life could not grow without death, while good could not flourish without evil. We are all regularly subject to negativity and unpleasant events, as well as good ones. What is important, however, is how we respond to these episodes.

"What counts is not what comes to you, rather how you respond to it," Epictetus famously stated.

It occurs to everyone; what counts is how you handle it. And, rather than having sympathy for yourself, you should choose a problem-solving mentality if you wish to live a fulfilling life and acquire your deepest goals.

Participate in Enjoyable Activities

When we do activities we enjoy, our frequency rises automatically. You may quickly shift your mood, raise your vibration, and entice even more of whatever you love by eating dishes you appreciate, seeing people you love, visiting destinations that brighten your heart, or participating in activities that give you joy.

We frequently assume that we must work hard to be happy, and we get so focused on our objectives that we neglect to cherish our lives. However, by demonstrating to the world that you value your days, you will draw even more happiness and comfort.

Make a Gratitude Book

One of the most effective methods to improve your vibration and employ the Law of Attraction is to appreciate what you currently have, and it's incredibly simple.

A thankfulness diary is just an option where you keep track of everything you're thankful for, including your house, the relationships in life, fitness, food, water, education, and so on.

You'll notice that you have a lot to be grateful for once you choose to practice gratitude.

Meditate

Meditation, like gratitude journals, is a simple and effective technique to boost your energy and elevate your vibration.

Meditating after journaling regarding your blessings, objectives, or strong affirmations, especially, may have a huge influence on your energy and attitude.

Love Yourself

Great manifest practitioners love and admire themselves. They embrace all of their errors and shortcomings and continue to move ahead despite setbacks.

Self-love is the most powerful manifestation signal you may give out to the world. Even while self-love is a long-term process, you may begin taking steps toward it right now.

Self-care and doing activities that make you happy don't have to be difficult or time-consuming. Even little practices may boost your frequency and lead to increased self-love and confidence.

The more you adore yourself, the more happiness will come your way.

Begin With Small Wishes

It's no more difficult to manifest anything significant than it is to manifest a cup of coffee. Most individuals, however, are unable to materialize as they attempt to attract significant things like a house or a large, unexpected payout before completely believing they can.

You destroy the Law of Attraction and also the manifestation procedure the moment you begin to doubt it.

You can't mislead the universe; it ultimately gives what you feel and believe. When you doubt that something will work, you ensure that it will not. Starting with minor manifestations and demonstrating that things operate is crucial in eliminating uncertainties before moving on to larger manifestations.

Practice Massive Motivated Action

It's all about taking deliberate action after deciding what you wish to attract. The cosmos will work with you rather than against you. The Law of Attraction may assist you in achieving your objectives more quickly, but you must still put in the effort. It's evident that lying on the sofa all day having ice cream and yearning for a healthy, slim physique won't work, no matter how strongly you think it.

5.6 Tips for Using the Law of Attraction

Several activities might assist you in learning how to apply the Law of Attraction in your own life. Here are a few suggestions:

- Journaling: Writing down your ideas may help you better understand your regular thinking patterns, determine if you are optimistic or pessimistic, and learn how to change pessimistic thought patterns.

- Put together a mood board: Make a visual recall to help you have a happy attitude. Stay inspired and focused on your objectives.

- Acceptance practice: Focus on embracing situations as they are rather than concentrating on what is wrong with the present or what has to be changed. It isn't to say you won't work for a better future; it just means you won't get caught up in yearning for circumstances to be better right now.

- Use affirmative self-talk: Set a goal to participate in positive self-talk every day if you suffer from being excessively critical of yourself. It might become easier with time, and you might find it increasingly difficult to sustain a negative perspective.

7 Signs
The Law Of Attraction
Is Working For You

1. You Are Aware Of Your Emotional Guidance System
2. You Feel Good When You Think Of Your Desire
3. You See Indicators
4. You'll Experience Synchronictties
5. Heightened Awareness Of Your Desires
6. You're Excited
7. You See Repeating Numbers Like 111, 11:11

5.7 The Role of the Law of Attraction in Manifestation

The Law of Attraction is the theory that guides us through manifesting our wishes and generating the life of our dreams. For instance, if we want to create a loving relationship, we must vibrate love in our energy, noting that like attracts like. To vibrate love, we should maintain our ideas and thinking patterns in a high vibration of affection. At the same time, by following the stages and instruments of manifestation, our vibrations may remain at a high level indefinitely; this is when manifestation takes place and we achieve our goal. Unfortunately, most of us have certain disruptive thinking habits in place that have been with us for a long time.

These ideas convince us we don't deserve our greatest desires and that we will never achieve our objectives, no matter how well we strive. The importance of the processes and instruments in the manifestation method stems from modifying these disruptive tendencies. Your goal is to strive to rise above and defeat negative ideas, replacing them with a new, more optimistic outlook.

Chapter 6: 3-6-9 Method of ManifeStation

There are several methods to start manifesting your wishes, from vision boards to dealing with attraction laws. The 369 approaches, in particular, have gotten a lot of attention recently, and it couldn't be simpler. It's natural to get disappointed early on the Law of Attraction journey. Perhaps you can't manage to manifest regardless of what you do, or you're constantly surrounded by negativity.

Whatever the impediment to manifestation may be, one technique to the entire method has a strong success record — the 3 6 9 methods.

It is a technique based on a paradigm of repeated and recurring ideas throughout our day. Its goal is to allow people to materialize or pull out from the Universe/God anything they wish. It is accomplished via specific and persistent affirmations that lead the subconscious to ponder that you already possess what you want. This manifestation approach gives you a new way to make your wildest aspirations a daily reality based on holy numerology.

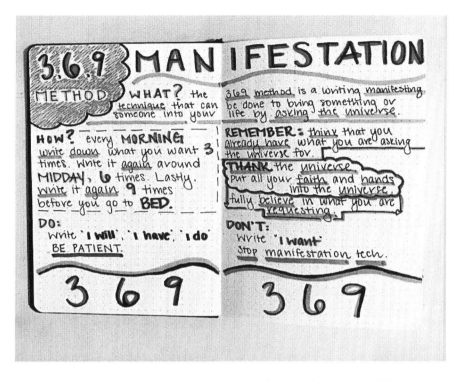

This chapter on the 369 manifestation technique will provide you with all the necessary information to get started.

We'll start by explaining the approach's efficacy and history before outlining a few simple and effective actions to begin practicing the 3 6 9 methods in everyday life.

Finally, we'll look at some more techniques that might help you maximize your manifestation potential.

6.1 Journaling for Manifestation

Manifestation opens our heart's work and gives a level of insight into our life that we may not have previously considered. We understand genuine appreciation, the necessity of self-reflection, and how being in the current moment may assist us in the sense of deep, enduring serenity when our hearts are fully open. As you'll see in this chapter, journaling allows you to achieve anything you want. Assuming we have what we need, penning

369

Shifting
Shifting
Shifting

I can shift easily I just have to fall asleep.
I can shift easily I just have to fall asleep.
I can shift easily I just have to fall asleep.
I can shift easily I just have to fall asleep.
I can shift easily I just have to fall asleep.
I can shift easily I just have to fall asleep.

I have shifted to hogwarts! I had so much fun dancing with Cedric and Luna. And listening to Luna sing was ethereal. I have fallen in love♡

I have shifted to hogwarts! I had so much fun dancing with Cedric and Luna. And listening to Luna sing was ethereal. I have fallen in love♡

regarding it in the present tense, and feeling the thankfulness that comes with obtaining our desires causes our energy to soar in a manifestation journaling exercise. Let's get started.

The written word has tremendous power. In your mind, pondering what to jot and why to write it has power. Taking a certain time to write in your diary once or twice a day helps you delve deep into your spirit and be honest about your deepest longings, whether physical items or states of being.

Journals are safe spaces where we may be completely honest with ourselves and anyone else. It's the same with manifesto journaling. The same kind of power may be found in writing out your greatest aspirations.

Continue to pen down in your diary about the stuff you would like to manifest, as well as review what you've previously written, to make those wishes even more real... and it is the goal. It must be tangible for anything to feel genuine in your mind and body.

"Esther Hicks, a specialist on the Law of Attraction, said via the nonphysical entity Abraham, who is the origin of her beliefs: "The main occasion has not been the manifestation; the main occasion has always been the method you think minute by minute since that's what life is." To manifest something, we must experience it in every bone of our being, and writing is the most efficient way to do so.

6.3 The Numerous Advantages of Using a Journal for Manifestation

One important advantage of writing down your wants and ideas in a notebook is that you may catch yourself and discover the prompts that generate negative thinking patterns when you read back over what you've written. This talent is quite useful in assisting you in changing your thinking regularly. It also helps you in identifying your keywords, phrases, or statements that may facilitate getting off that pessimistic track and back into the land of optimistic thinking.

Another significant advantage of maintaining a manifestation notebook is the capacity to stay in the current moment. As you jot and contemplate, you realize that this now, right now, is ideal, and joy, calm, and fulfillment are all freely available in this instant. This discovery is a pivotal moment in the process. The capacity to remain in the present moment is transformative because it allows us to see that the past is over and the future hasn't arrived yet. Living "at the moment" reminds us that we already have all we require.

Concentrate Your Thoughts

When you start journaling and writing down your thoughts, dreams, feelings, goals, and objectives, you'll notice that simply writing them down on paper helps you concentrate your mind to make you feel more resolved, motivated, and focused. You will have a deeper understanding of yourself and why you need what you seek. This kind of total attention is invaluable when you're in the creative phase of manifestation.

List Down the Objectives

Becoming 100% focused might be intimidating for some people. There are several possibilities! Making a list (a lengthy one!) in your notebook is one approach to discovering your innermost wishes. As you continue to write, your concepts will be clearer, and you'll be able to narrow down exactly what you like to create. At some time, it will be as if a light bulb would go off, and you'll have that "aha" moment. At this stage, your gut will notify you that it's correct and you've discovered what you're looking for.

List Down Your Goals

Evaluate what you want to achieve out of manifesting psychologically and emotionally as you analyze your manifestation objectives. When you consider what you need to add to your life, your desire's mental and emotional reasons can be enlightening. Again, opening yourself and devoting your soul and heart to this practice might lead you down various routes to genuine happiness and fulfillment. Changing your goals in this way can only result in full pleasure with the outcome. It is about achieving actual, long-term, and complete happiness with yourself and your life.

Show Your Appreciation

As you've learned, expressing thankfulness for all the wonderful things in your life daily assists you be present in the moment. Reading what you've written in your notebook somehow makes it more solid and real, resulting in unexpected and even deeper feelings of gratitude for your life as it is—at the moment. This unexpected advantage of writing may take you off guard, but you will be eternally thankful for what you learn regarding yourself, your family and friends, and your life as a result. Gratitude has the power to transform lives.

Self-Examination and Self-Discovery

Educating yourself to put down your inner wishes and ideas in a notebook might lead to major epiphanies regarding who you are. Journaling may help you determine what you want out of life, and it's a great way to get to the bottom of your sentiments. Writing in your diary may help you figure out who you are and what you want to be in this society. Another unexpected benefit of writing is that it helps in your effort to transform your life into one of total pleasure and joy.

Keep a Journal of Your Journey

As you proceed through this life-changing trip, keep a record of your accomplishments and problems and any new or unusual insights you might have. Being honest with yourself and without holding anything back can assist you in reflecting on your development afterward.

Understanding that the goal of this method is to decompose your old, boring, negative habits and methods of thinking to replace them with new, constructive, and strong thought patterns will lead to successful manifestation! Time for Manifestation to Work

The Law of Attraction, a strong global law that can entice everything you wish, is comparable to the 369 manifestation technique. Everyone can harness and use the Law of Attraction to their advantage.

6.4 Concept of 369 Method

Jotting down what you intend to manifest 3 times in the mornings, 6 times during the daytime, and 9 times in the nighttime is a component of the 369 technique.

This approach grew popular on TikTok, with the videos with the hashtags "369methods" hoarding over 175 million views. It's not hard to find people on the application who say the tactic has helped them in manifesting new associations, significant quantities of cash, and further things.

Nikola Tesla, a well-known inventor, had faith that figures 3, 6, and 9 were potent figures for establishing in the 20th century. "Tesla felt these holy figures were the solution to accessing the cosmos," spiritual counselor Diana Zalucky says.

Besides the figures, the 369 exercise trails the Law of Attraction, which clasps that we entice what we focus on.

Ms. Shaunaa Cummins, hypnotist and author of Wish Craft, says that concentrating on what you wish, exclusively regular, may aid your brain "find what it's looking for, and therefore [become] more likely to draw your desires into action."

6.5 History of 369 Method

As previously stated, this technique is based on Nicola Tesla's 369 code, which is sometimes referred to as his "secret code" and is linked to our power to control reality.

Because of the rule, they represent in our numbers system, and Tesla dubbed these heavenly numbers unbreakable. Keep in mind that a round shape has 360 degrees and that 3 + 6 equals 9.

Meanwhile, no matter how many times you split this circle, you always end up with the numbers 3, 6, or 9. Although Tesla was a math genius who published more on the subject, these are the main facts you should be aware of, and they teach you everything you intend to learn about the importance of these digits in our world.

We have excellent cause to respect Tesla's work: he established the present alternating current (AC) electrical delivery system, among other things, and he continued to develop new technologies throughout his life.

Chapter 7: Method and TipS For 3-6-9 Method

This chapter will discuss the methods and tips on the 369 Manifestation Technique

7.1 Steps to Use the 369 Method

Of course, before you begin, you'll need to decide exactly what you intend to manifest. Once you've figured it out, it's time to craft an affirmation. (If you wished to manifest money, for instance, your affirmation might be "I will get a significant quantity of money.")

- Get a paper and pen and use this strategy as soon as you get up. "I am really glad for my employment at _____" is a sample statement comparable to the one I am now using. "It goes above my expectations, and I am handled with respect and prefer my work. I'm ecstatic to have the opportunity to pursue my passion for every day in a profession that pays well. I like the fact that my boss and the team think highly of me." You can ask for particular sums of money, a certain location, perks, or a particular position. The more precise you can be, the better.

- You'll write an identical sentence three   times each morning, and you'll try to avoid some other interruptions. You must remain concentrated and reach a zone where you're on the receiving frequency.

- This message's length of seventeen seconds is critical. As per Abraham Hicks, a manifestation master and law of attraction specialist, it takes seventeen seconds of pure concentration to start the manifestation process. We should not question our aspirations or let any doubt seep in within these seventeen seconds. It will undermine the energy and accomplish nothing. Practice makes flawless, even if it's difficult at first.

- If your mind wanders throughout these seventeen seconds, don't become irritated. Also, avoid nurturing any thoughts of obsession or underpinning feelings of inadequacy. If you can't control your doubts, you'll generate resistance, and all your time and effort will be for naught. Take a step back, calm yourself, and resume chanting your affirmations after you've reached a state of neutrality.

- You will ultimately, and sometimes soon, sense what you are seeking (the Universe/God/Source/ etc.) will happen to you. If you're new to purposeful manifestation, you'll quickly learn the difference between sensations of lack and a deep understanding that your wishes will be realized in the heart.

- It's simple to overlook our manifestations in the afternoon, in the stress of our day. It might sometimes be difficult to get into a good frame of mind and focus on the frequency we want to be in. One of the most beneficial aspects of this approach is that it teaches us how to reach and maintain high-frequency vibrations during the day. It will assist us in staying on pace to manifest more swiftly in general.

- The more we reiterate those affirmations, the quicker our subconscious accepts them as true. You must jot down the same sentence from the morning six times at this point in the day. Don't rush; make it a routine of your regular self-care practice. You can repeat the phrases 6 times out loudly (with enthusiasm, not desperation!) once you've written them down. Assure yourself that you want and will get the reality you want.

- Before you lay your head down for the night, take out your journal and repeat this affirmation nine times. After that, you'll recite it nine times loudly right before going to bed. It is such an important phase because our brain consolidates what it has learned throughout the day when we sleep. We should take advantage of the opportunity to allow those thoughts to rest in our minds undisturbed with no external interruptions that might potentially impact our vibration. When used correctly, it may be a fast track to reprogramming your mind.

- We use the 3–6–9 approach to rewire our thoughts. It's acceptable and natural to have a mind free of aggressively repressive and doubting ideas when we first start this new exercise. On the other hand, our brain cannot discern the differences between memories, dreams, or something wholly thought up only since we want to like it when we imagine constantly. When we confirm and imagine without opposition, the notion is allowed to stay in our brains.

- You must do your best to remain in harmony when using the 3–6–9 approach and continue pouring the energy to build the lifestyle you wish. You must maintain a frequency of receiving and trusting that you will receive what you have asked for. It might be challenging at times, particularly when you're attempting to manifest things you need or desire, such as a job, a vehicle, money, or indeed a relationship. However, to keep yourself feeling positive, it's a good idea to repeat your learned affirmation throughout the day. You are on a level to receive and accept once you are on an optimistic or even neutral frequency. Get pumped! (However, don't get too pleased that you start to feel resentful.)

7.2 Points to Remember

When using the 369 methods to materialize, keep in mind a few things.

Time Constraints

If you're a novice at manifestation, it's crucial not to put too much pressure on your manifestation to materialize as you want it to. No matter how confident you might manifest by that precise date, it will elicit opposition and put you into a hopeless vibration. When I'm manifesting, I seldom give it a time frame; instead, I state that God will fulfill my desires in its own time.

That isn't to imply that something can't be manifested in as little as a few days. I trust the Lord with that! Don't be hesitant to seek a signal that the desired manifestation is on the route to you while using this or other law of attraction techniques.

Time does not exist when we appear. Time is only a social concept since everything that occurs is the present moment. Suppose you think about the time of your manifestation and allow it to enter your consciousness. In that case, you're indicating to the Universe that you'll manifest something or the other in the future and that you're now waiting for it to happen. We stay linked with our goals and inform our subconscious that we have it when we remove any perception of time from the issue and experience the sensations of having it now. Don't look at the time. You may be assured that it is on the road to you. Your desires are yearning for you to receive them with welcoming hands in your vortex.

Power Is All Yours

In one of her books, The Power Is Within You, Louise Hay, an American inspirational author, discusses the potential of luring all of your wishes. She likens manifesting anything into our lives, like placing a restaurant order. You put your order exactly how you want it, and you do not doubt that the chef is cooking it right now in the kitchen. The dinner will be served when it is done, and you are looking forward to it. You are not concerned or worried that the cook has forgotten about the food and that it might never arrive. You're positive it will happen eventually.

As we transmit our demand up to the Divine kitchen, we must understand that, just as our food arrives when it's ready, our wishes arrive when they're ready, and you're eager to receive them.

Self-doubt and unpleasant emotions will resurface from time to time. It's just the way we're wired. Few individuals are ecstatic throughout the entirety of the day, every day. Those who are likely to meditate frequently invest much in their spiritual and mental growth. Regardless, those sensations will surface apparently out of nowhere. Notice how you think and then release/transmute the ick is the easiest technique to combat these emotions and stay connected on receiving frequency.

Keep your vibrations up, your objectives clear and significant, and your practice consistent.

7.3 Tips For 369 Manifestation Technique

Below we mention some beneficial tips for manifestation.

1. Always talk in the present tense, as if your manifestation has already happened. When you say things like "I will" or "I want," you're telling the universe that you don't have what you want, which causes nature to give you more about what you don't have.

2. Do not stress over your manifestation. As previously stated, think in the present tense and realize that this manifestation is all yours; it simply hasn't come yet. The when and how are not your concerns; it's where divine timing and faith in the universe come into play, knowing that once your vibration is ready to accept your wish, it will be given to you.

3. Have faith that your manifestation will show up before the 33 days are through! Your desires will surface once you are prepared to embrace them, once again thanks to the divine arrangement. If you've made it to the completion of the 33 days, but still haven't seen magic, don't give up. Release it into the cosmos and trust that it will be yours shortly since you have assumed it!

4. Maintain a steady pace. To make this work, you should set aside time every day to write three times in the morning, six times during the day, and nine times before bed. Set the alarm so you don't miss it, and plan to take this seriously in your calendar. You will not be regretful, I assure you.

5. If you experience pessimism or self-doubt when using the 369 manifestation technique, you may find it difficult to connect your energies to what you desire. When you have doubts, take a break from the process and jot down what they are. Is it a fact or a belief? Can you manage your doubt and make a change, or would you need to let go of something you can't control? Is it possible to reinterpret it in some way? People's barriers to manifesting money might appear; therefore, the trick is to feel connected

with the sum you want to attract. Would you stay in the energy of manifesting $ 1000 if you can't even stay in the energy of manifesting $ 10,000? And then repeat this process till you've reached your total requirement. Allow yourself to recover.

7.4 The Importance of Numbers

You might have the secret to the cosmos if you only understood the majesty of the 3, 6, and 9. The Universe is directly related to the synchronization of these specific numbers. The 3 number is a direct connection to the Source/Universe. The number six indicates our most inner power. Nine is associated with going on from the past and helps in the removal of any self-doubt or pessimism.

I had never heard of this practice until recently from a friend, even though I have been applying the Law of Attraction daily for almost five years. I'm not sure how much I understand the importance of the digits, but I consider myself ready for new experiences. As a result, I don't believe I must accord with every facet of an ideology. I'm happy with taking bits and bobs from a concept that may help me and improve my overall well-being, whether it's new to me or not. According to Zalucky, the 369 approach combines numbers and the Law of Attraction. The meaning of each number in the sequence is as follows:

Only a few brilliant minds have attempted to solve this riddle, including Marko Rodin, the creator of Rodin Coil and Vortex Mathematics, and John Ernst Worrell Keely, the man who discovered the Sympathetic Vibratory Physics, who wrote: "thirds, sixths, and ninths, were incredibly potent" and "molecular depersonalization or dissolution of both basic and composite elements, whether liquid and gas or solid, a flow of vibrational antagonistic thirds, sixths, To acquire the optimum results in the dissolution of water, the instrument is placed on thirds, sixths, and ninths."

- 3 signifies our creative self-expression and connection to the origin of the cosmos;

- 6 represents our inner power and peace.

- 9 symbolizes our inner regeneration (as in letting go of what no longer serves us and changing into who we are becoming)

Let's take a closer look at the meaning of those figures.

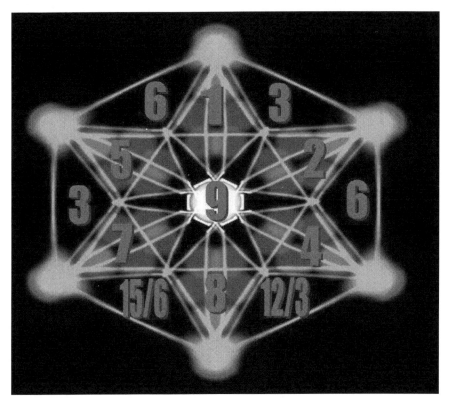

Number Three

The magic starts with the number three, representing the foundation of Formation, the Sources, the feminine, and primitive syntropy. "The triangle is the most fundamental unit of all construction," Buckminster Fuller said, "and the tetrahedron is an essential structure of energy dynamics." "Triangle Planck oscillators form the thread of time and space, or information of the space memory structure powering the growth of our global dynamics," according to Nassim Harameinand, the Resonance Academy.

The Tripod of Life, also known as the Borromean rings, represents the energy pattern of the second day of creation, and the core of the Seed of Life, which is thought to hold the patterns of formation, and the shapes of space and time, according to ancient teachings of Sacred Geometry. It's also said that simply gazing at these holy patterns helps heal and extend our minds. Energy is created and expelled when three third-dimensional rings overlap to form the Tripod of Life shape. This energy can help us be more creative and expand our awareness.

The Law of Three is a guideline that highlights the strength and efficacy of digit three. Everything that arrives in threes is complete and perfect, according to the Latin idea "Omnetrium perfectum." Nowadays, it is employed in various fields, including literature, photography, cinema, and advertising.

Number Six

The number six is its twin and everlasting partner in connection to the initial number (3), signifying the beginning of global dualism, the principle of Genders, the feminine and masculine energies as parts of the total, the Yin/Yang, and Vesica Piscis. Growth begins with the number 6, and entropy generates everything we can see. It is the male side of energy and general creation and one of the cornerstones of the manifestation of cosmic awareness.

Number Nine

The apex, the gem of the groups of three, the triple times three, the Mathematical Fingerprint of God, is the number nine. It has heavenly importance, representing the singularity, the beginning of all, and the vacuum, everything but nothing. Symbolizes the Seed of Life, a sign of reproduction and creation consisting of eight spheres and the blueprint for the cosmos and life. "Dark Matter, the mysterious particle in the cosmos, is represented by the number nine." - Rodin, Marko. Even though the 9 signifies the whole, the Soul, the 3 + 6, our whole cosmos manifests in 3s and 6s. When you multiply three by two, you get six, but when you multiply six by two, you get twelve (12, 1+2=3), which brings us back to three. The doubling of twelve becomes twenty-four (24, 2+4=6), and so on.

Chapter 8: TeStimonialS and SucceSS StorieS of CelebritieS and Common People

The magic of appreciation is shining brightly, and one tale after another is unfolding.

These remarkable people use the power of thankfulness to influence the Universe to help them achieve their goals. This collection of Magical Success tales chronicles the lives of extraordinary people who use magic to achieve their goals. These genuine tales demonstrate that anyone can alter their life only a few times if they want to. These beautiful people's fantastic trip continued.

In this chapter, you'll read Law of Attraction True Life Stories about career success, pursuing a passion, finding happiness, attracting money, receiving medals, and more. All of this was made possible in just a short period through the power of thankfulness.

These tales describe how these supernatural beings gratefully fulfill their wishes. I am confident that these inspiring, miraculous success tales will inspire you to pursue your goals.

Remember that nothing is hard if you attempt; nevertheless, nothing will happen unless you begin.

Sarah Regan- Spirituality and Relationship Writer

If you're wondering if the 369 approach works, you're not alone. I had to give it a shot myself. I decided to start with anything easy and uplifting, so I chose "I am overwhelmed with appreciation every day" as my affirmation.

I can't tell whether this strategy would inspire a romantic lead to text you or gain you a promotion at work, but I can claim that writing out my feelings of thankfulness made me feel better.

I discovered I was continuously feeling more optimistic and noticed things I appreciated the day after using the 369 approaches for approximately a week.

It's as if my brain is now searching for reasons to be grateful for supporting the notion I've been teaching. It's fascinating stuff, and it illustrates, in my opinion, that giving certain concepts more consideration than others is worth it.

Kristen Rouse- A law of Attraction Practitioner

"Whether you believe that you can or you can't, you are correct." It is a quote that I nearly always think about. It reminds me that our ideas give the Law of Attraction its strength. I may choose the most effective manifestation strategy. I may jot the most thorough and positive affirmation in the world, but if I don't trust it or don't trust myself, I won't be able to attract it. Then it's pointless. The same may be said of your involvement with the 369 approaches. I've tried it myself, and I assure you that it works. It assisted me manifest because I believe in it. Don't give up; I wasn't always like this. In truth, I've only been a fan for a few months. Before then, I believed that remedies that functioned for others would not work for me. But it didn't take long for me to see how damaging this mode of thinking was. I questioned myself about the appropriate things about myself and my desires. Do I want to be miserable for my entire life, or do I want to alter my way of thinking? Now I feel that things will work out for me and achieve my goals. I'm hoping for nice things and new experiences. So, okay, do the same. Don't be surprised if miracles occur. It is your inherent right to get what you desire, and it is only you and your ideas preventing you from getting it. Let go of those negative ideas and trust that things will work out for you.

You must perform it for three weeks, or twenty-one days. Perhaps this is why it isn't helping you. Give it another attempt, but this time you should be persistent and stick with it for the entire 21-day period. This time, don't allow negative ideas to get in the way of your manifestation.

Kabir and the Law of Attraction

At six, Kabir discovered his calling as a magician after seeing the world's finest magician, David Copperfield, appear on television in Malaysia. His love developed as he grew older, and he could no longer sustain it as a pastime.

When he got his hands on a copy of The Success Principles, he was clearer than ever that he wanted to be the Local David Copperfield.

The mind is a strong, and some could even say miraculous, tool. Acting as if, as I like to put it, is a huge aspect of The Law of Attraction. The cosmos will respond to your energies if you act as if you're exactly where you wish to be.

"How would I act if I were a world-famous magician?" he wondered.

As a result, he adopted that manner and created a vision board.

He followed me out and told me about his ambitions to learn and perform in America. Instead of stating, "I would like to study magic in America," I suggested to him, "I am learning magic in America."

He altered his vision board even more to reflect this. He was capable of attracting a wealthy Chinese person into business via a mastermind group who was willing to sponsor him to learn magic in America thanks to his new perspective, tenacity, and vibrations.

To add to his vision board, he had a buddy draw up a newspaper item with the heading "Malaysian Magician to Appear in Hollywood."

You can probably predict what occurred next. He was asked to perform at The Magic Castle in Hollywood after a year of envisioning and executing unconventional activities.

Daniel and the Law of Attraction

Daniel realized the power of his thoughts, objectives, and attention on a whole new level after viewing the film The Secret and hearing me explain the Law of Attraction. He chose to use it to build his dream home in Maui. When it was on sale, he made the greatest offer he could, but it was quite low that the bank didn't even respond.

Because the top bidder could not complete the transaction, the bank reduced the house's price.

Daniel thought hard about what he could pay and what he thought was a reasonable deal for his family, which turned out to be too low.

"Everything you desire wants you, too," I told him and his family, "but you have to act immediately to acquire it." As bizarre as it may seem to many people, he and his family began a visualization exercise. They would travel up to the house's driveway almost every day, park, and act as if it were theirs.

He'd say hello to his family as if he were returning home from work, they'd plot where the furniture would go, and they'd sit on the back deck, looking at the horse enclosure, imagining their horse living with them again, rather than being boarded at a neighboring stable.

After reading The Success Principles, he became even more convinced. He was confident that he was on the right course. He no longer felt concerned or obsessive after spending to get the house examined before the second auction. He felt peaceful and at ease, believing he was doing all he could to obtain the property.

So, what exactly do we know?

The greatest bid fell through again, and the bank asked if he could boost his price by $15,000, which he agreed to do. Daniel held firm in his proposal, claiming that it was the best price for his family. A few weeks later, he got a call; the bank had approved his offer!

Sharon and the Law of Attraction

Sharon became a firm believer in The Law after seeing The Secret while enjoying pizza and hearing about my tale of putting a $100,000 check for the money I intended to manifest within 12 months above my mattress.

She declared to the cosmos that the next time she ate pizza would be on April 1st, her birthday, around 1 p.m. in Venice, Italy.

You could imagine what kind of hardship it was for her because she adored pizza! She began informing everyone about her desire, unconcerned whether they thought she was insane since she knew it would be fulfilled. She made a vision board of Venice's waterways and put a photo of a window facing a balcony and a canal from the resort she planned to stay at.

When she decided to visit Venice in January that year, someone she had met previously and who had heard of her desire volunteered to provide her a visa to Venice with no conditions attached. She felt uneasy after finding the hotel she sought was booked for a conference but she called again one week later and found a room available. It turned out that this was the place where the vision board's precise photo was taken.

Oprah Winfrey

"You receive what you possess the guts to ask for in life."

"Be grateful for whatever you have; you will eventually have more. You will never have sufficient if you focus on what you don't have."

When talking about Law of Attraction success stories, it's nearly hard to overlook Oprah. She's spoken openly about how the law contributed to her success. In an interview featuring Larry King, she explained how the Law of Attraction assisted her in landing her dream part of Sophie in the film 'The Color Purple' and how this paved the way for her great career in show business.

'The Secret,' a documentary film, was promoted on Oprah's show. The film focuses on how the Law of Attraction assisted many people in achieving their goals. It's presented in the form of a sequence of interviews. Oprah is responsible for the concept's recent resurgence. Her broadcasts devoted to the film attracted a large audience and helped sales of the film's companion book.

Oprah has given countless interviews throughout the years

about using Law of Attraction strategies to change people's lives. She has also supported writers that believe in the Law of Attraction, such as Eckhart Tolle.

Lady Gaga

"Positive affirmations cause your subconscious thought to lure success and help you live a better life."

"Music is my passion," she says. "I can achieve stardom. I'm going to record a number one album with number one singles. It isn't yet; it is a deception. Over and over, you're telling a falsehood. Then one day, the falsehood is proven to be real." She was only a striving artist with lofty ambitions. She has become one of the most well-known and rich pop performers globally. She could do so by concentrating on what she aspired to become instead of where she was at the time. Lady Gaga transformed her life through the Law of Attraction tactics of visualization, affirmations, and mantras. She utilized certain terms to persuade her brain that she was already well-known. "It's almost like a chant. You tell yourself that every day," she explains.

Jay Z

"I think you have the ability to manifest things via your words."

"You make your luck," a wise gentleman once told me. "Luck isn't this supernatural spirit that dances about the globe randomly, giving pleasure and joy to people." Jay Z credits his rapid climb from not-so-pleasant initial periods to fortune and prominence today to Law of Attraction practices. He believes that blaming people for your bad luck would lead you nowhere. He is a great believer in taking control of your future. He began believing in his abilities. He trusted in his ability and exploited it to attain his goals.

"Making music is an artistic endeavor. It makes no difference to who and what you are as an individual. It does not imply that you are entitled to or above the law. People are still treated as human beings by you. It does not affect the universe's rules. There is a balance in life, and every action has a consequence. So, if you give out bad energy, you will receive negative vibes in return. You must live your life following the rules of the universe, and I haven't forgotten that." Jay Z

Kanye West

"I am a product of my own making. I was certain that I was the greatest rapper on the planet. I sat and pondered it, and suddenly I transformed into Kanye West. I've always had the impression that I could do anything." That is the primary means through which people are manipulated! Their impression of themselves is based on their thoughts! Their perspective of themselves slows them down. If you've been taught that you can't accomplish anything, you won't. "I was raised to believe that I was capable of doing anything. And my name is Kanye West, and I'm 36 years old." You can't overlook him, whether you like him or not. For your information, Kanye West is a rapper. The successful rapper did not come from a family of rappers. His self-belief is responsible for his meteoric rise in money. He claims that you must become your own biggest cheerleader. You must first root for yourself if you want people to root for you.

To achieve your goals, you must concentrate on who you wish to be rather than your current situation. Kanye attributes his incredible accomplishment to his imagination and unwavering faith.

Jim Carrey

"As far as I could tell, it's just a matter of telling the world what you need and then striving toward it and letting go as to how it manifests. I'm a total believer. I believe in the power of manifestation. I believe in launching a desired rocket into the universe. When you feel you have it, you receive it. When it's going to come, when it's going to arrive, people continue to say. And that's the incorrect way to go about it. You're turning your back on it. Here it is, here it is, here it is, you must say."

"Many of us chose our paths out of fear masquerading as practicality. We never bother to ask the cosmos for what we desire since it seems impossible to obtain. I'm living evidence that you can get what you want from the cosmos." One of Hollywood's top comedians, Jim Carrey, is a firm believer in the Law of Attraction. He has stated publicly that he owes his rags-to-riches rise in fortune to the law. Jim Carrey explains how he utilized intention and vision to become a billionaire and then start a fantastic career in the film business in a conversation with Oprah.

Will Smith

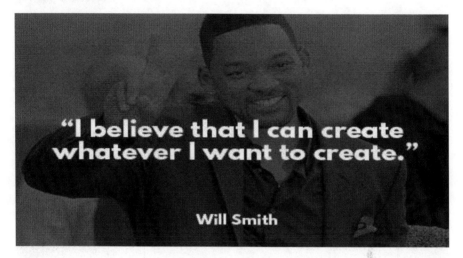

"I feel I have the ability to create whatever I choose. If I can apply my mind to it, study it, discover the patterns, and — it's difficult to put into words. It's true philosophical, esoteric gibberish, but I believe that we are who we choose; to be. In the Universe, our thoughts, feelings, dreams, and ideas are physical. What if we imagine anything? It gives it a tangible push toward realization, which we might send into the cosmos." The legendary Hollywood actor Will Smith has said openly that the Law of Attraction tactics are responsible for his immense success. He emphasizes the importance of self-belief in getting where you want to go. Will Smith, unlike many others, is aware of the legislation and takes advantage of every chance to disseminate the word. He has stated several times that success is within everyone's reach; all they have to do is trust it. He emphasizes that all you have to do is determine what you want, and the Universe will handle the rest.

Arnold Schwarzenegger

"I'm aiming to be the highest-grossing movie star in the world. You develop a vision of who you wish to be and then live your life as if that vision were already true. Ever since I was a child, I saw myself as being and having whatever it was that I desired. I never had any reservations in my mind about it. The human intellect is quite amazing. I moved around the event as I owned it after getting my first Mr. Universe title. I have already chosen the title. I'd won it several times in my head that there was no question in my thoughts that I'd win it this time. Then it happened again when I went to the movies. I saw myself as a well-known actor who made a lot of money. I sensed and tasted success. It was only a matter of time until it all came to pass." Arnold Schwarzenegger credits his success in various professions, including weightlifting, acting, and politics, to vision, belief, focus, and visualization.

Steve Harvey

"Like attracts like. You must realize that you will be a magnet. That's what you attract to you, whatever you are. If you're pessimistic, you'll attract pessimism. Are you confident? You are an optimistic thinker. You're a kind person, right? The majority of people are nice to you... You can hold anything in your hand

if you picture it in your imagination. It is correct. Outside of the Bible, [The Secret] is by far the most compelling book I've ever read." Steve Harvey, a self-proclaimed believer in the Law of Attraction, has actively pushed the notion on his talk program. He, like Oprah, had a major role in the popularity of the film "The Secret" and, later, the book of the same name.

Steve Harvey has often remarked that the Law of Attraction tactics encourage him to achieve his goals. Your success, he claims, is certain if you learn the technique of asking, believing, and receiving, as well as exercising visualization and thankfulness.

Mandy's Story

I was evicted from my house because my spouse failed to pay his mortgage. As a result, the agencies refused to retain me unless I paid six months' rent up ahead, which I didn't afford. I was needy and had a 4-year-old daughter, but I had faith something might pop up. I saw myself receiving the keys to the new house while sitting in my chair. I drove about for a few days, and behold and surprise, and there was a lovely small cottage with a sign outside stating "rent." When I phoned, the gentleman stated he'd be there in 1 hour to tour you around. That day, the keys were handed over to me, and we spent the next seven years there happily.

Diana's Story

One of the toughest years of my life was 2017. I'd broken up with my now-ex-husband and was focusing on my favorite therapy method (the only option that appeared to help me feel better): exercise. At least, it was until I hurt my back early that year. Except that I couldn't lean down without difficulty; it was a minor ailment. I felt alright walking around, but I couldn't perform my favorite routines. There would be no Zumba, yoga, or strength training. And, by tapping into the woo, I was able to overcome all of that and even return to instructing Zumba. The most difficult obstacle I had was conquering the daily mental fight I faced. My stamina was already low because of the painful life experience I was processing. It was just another setback. It would be so simple to sink further and deeper into depression. But I understood that giving in to the bad energy would prolong my confinement. Or maybe indefinitely. And I wasn't going to allow a few negative incidents in my life to spoil the rest of my life!

Fortunately, I had some prior understanding of The Universe, manifesting, as well as the Law of Attraction. I realized I could work on my thoughts and energies because I couldn't concentrate on my body. So, I tried, and that wasn't easy, but I continued.

I knew I'd be able to get through it! The Law of Attraction tactics that I use successfully are listed below.

- Don't Give In: Keep your thinking optimistic and firm, be open to mending - mentally (meditation) and physically (rest yoga), and keep your vibrations high.
- Scripting: Journal in the present tense as if what you desire has already occurred.
- Intentional Action: Take action that moves you closer to your goal and ensures that those efforts are connected with what you want – I underwent physical therapy and afterward self-training.

- Vision Board: Create a vision board that is particular to your recovery / a specific area of your life.

Over time, I regained my stamina as well as my self-assurance. Even better, I'm back to instructing Zumba! Woop! Everything on my vision board for recovery came true!

Nadia Simpson

"I initially became interested in manifestations due to the film and booked The Secret. My elder brother presented this movie to me, and I watched it every evening during my first semester at university. It motivated me to establish my goals, and while I was in my second semester, I made my first vision board. I printed photos of stuff I wished to implement in the long run and the near term. I had an image of Fortune magazine on my vision board at the time, with my business logo glued on the bottom. I was only an undergraduate with no extensive network, so I had no idea how I'd land a Forbes feature, but I was confident that I would. I hung the board over my bed so I could see it each morning. I began attending networking events. Before Covid, I met folks who learned how to connect and contact media. As a result, I managed to see a Forbes editor and proposed my socially progressive company to her."

"Manifesting trained me to stop worrying about how to achieve what I need and to realize with every cell of my being that I am the maker of my reality."

Athavia Dimple

"When I was employed for organizations as a beverages industry executive, I usually found it frustrating to provide comments or proposals to the corporate executives. They always made it challenging to incorporate the thoughts into their pre-determined structure. As a result, I realized I had an entrepreneur's attitude. It was as if a door opened when I began to consider myself a business owner, and behind it was a kingdom of limitless possibilities! I then created my whole company from the ground up, including the company name, website colors, appearance and feel, commodities, ideal consumers, and how it would expand in the future. Consequently, I've started a company called All Things Drinks."

Nicola Geismar

"I started manifesting because I was conscious of my restricting barriers and beliefs that continued surfacing over time. I became interested in these ideas and discovered that while you might desire anything on a conscious level, the subconscious has the true power. And that's usually what's keeping you back. Affirmations and optimistic thinking are simply two parts of the puzzle for me. It helps the subconscious reprogram new ideas through meditating, embodied energetic movement practice, and hypnosis. Since starting this path, I've manifested a vacation to the Caribbean, linked with ideal customers, and obtained professional contracts and workshops on international stages."

Jo Threlfall

"I was recuperating and reading a lot regarding mindfulness after a cervix cancer treatment and operations. During my rehabilitation period, I started reading Vex King's Good Times and Good Vibes, which truly drew my attention to spirituality. It taught me that my ideas were in charge of my destiny and that manifesting via journaling and visualization could assist me in obtaining anything I wanted. I delved into the Law of Attraction and began to understand more about manifestation and put it to practice to check how it worked. I've learned to let go of bad energy and appreciate what I have. I began to appreciate life more by living in the present and accepting each day as it came. I obtained my ideal job and developed my staff by adopting this approach. I discovered my dream apartment in Manchester and now reside in a town I enjoy. I obtained the job after advertising on LinkedIn just after my cervical treatment was completed. I received a DM and was offered the position two days later. It all occurred so fast, and the organization I work for is named Embryo, which is ironic given what happened to me health-wise in 2020."

Inbaal

"I have manifested my wonderful career as a clairvoyant with many TV appearances over the past two decades. I discovered my spouse to my very exact criteria, such as zodiac sign and hair color, she says. I was the astrologer at Elle magazine, used to have a regular radio stint on talkSPORT radio, and more. Despite being told I was infertile, I gave birth to four children. I dropped nine pounds. During the financial crisis, I purchased and sold houses. I now instruct folks how to manifest as well."

Elizabeth's   Story

My mum has a manifesting box in her room. It's merely a shoebox decorated with Christmas gift paper leftovers. It appears to be a kaleidoscope of prior Christmases. She's been using it for approximately 10 years and has had great success with it. She tossed in several photographs of stuff she'd want in a house the first time she used it. She created a home with everything she desired, but not exactly as she had imagined. For instance, she needed a library with built-in bookshelves, so she put a photo of one into her manifestation box. Her lounge room chimney now has a simple built-in bookcase, which isn't the same as a library. She quickly discovered that while putting items in her manifestation box, she needed to be as specific as possible...just like with everything else you desire to manifest.

My mother's manifestation box helps since it assists her in overcoming any barriers to manifesting her wishes. She'll put stuff in there that she wouldn't ordinarily consider conceivable, but it helps because it removes her barrier.

She utilized her manifesting box to land a new workplace a few years ago. And she was a huge success! She visualized the company she desired, the area, the precise position, and even a significant pay raise. The firm even reached out to her to ask if she was interested in working with them. It took her barely six weeks to appear.

She decided to give it another shot this year in the hopes of landing a new career. She produced a list explaining exactly what she needed in her new position (e.g., a significant income rise, what it would be like to perform there, etc.). She stuffed her manifesto list inside her manifesting box and then forgot about it.

She has the position she requested, but it isn't quite what she had hoped for. Yes, her compensation grew by the amount she desired, and she now only needs to work four days per week, but she overlooked one crucial factor.

What exactly is the issue? She works for the same business as me. Yes, the job, position, and organization are all the same; the only difference is that there are fewer hours in the office and more money. Other than that, nothing has changed.

What was it that she desired? New employment at a different firm with less work and higher pay. You might be asking why she's whining when she has a nice job, but she chose to work anywhere else.

My mother never requested her supervisor if she might work fewer hours a week since the manifesting box worked so wonderfully. "Traffic has been so horrible recently," he said, "why don't you work at home three days a week?" She never begged for extra money from him. It was just handed to her. How long does it take you? It's been three weeks.

However, she's back to square one. Less labor and even more money are insufficient to persuade her to continue. She wanted to ensure she won't leave anything out this time as she presented her request to the Lord in the manifesting box. She didn't just take it for granted that the Universe knew what she wanted.

Do you know what the most enjoyable aspect is?

She has an appointment at a different firm for a new position only after one week, which pays much more.

So, yep, this manifesting thing is effective. All you have to do now is get clear on what you need, request it, and let it happen. Try the manifesting box method if you're having trouble getting things done. For my mum, it worked.

Denzel Washington

"You entice what you think, who you are, and what you attract, both positively and adverse." Denzel Hayes Washington Jr. is a producer, director, and actor from the United States. He's already discussed the Law of Attraction and how he feels we draw things through our thoughts.

He claims that whatever our feelings and thoughts are concentrated on, whether anxiety or excitement, good or bad, we will draw into our lives.

Andrew Carnegie

"You are who you think you are. Think large, feel big, act good, strive big, donate big, apologize big, laugh big, love big." Andrew Carnegie, a Scottish-American industrialist, was born in the United States. He is often regarded as one of the wealthiest persons and Americans of all time, having guided the creation of the U.S. steel market in the late nineteenth century. Throughout his life, he was incredibly wealthy, and he donated approximately $310 million to foundations, charities, and institutions. Andrew Carnegie thought that the mind is incredibly strong and can employ that power in our lives once we channel our belief system.

Russell Brand

"Believing in oneself is tough since the self-concept is an imaginary concept. You are, in reality, a part of the Universe's beautiful oneness. Everything lovely in the world is contained within you." Russell Edward Brand is an actor, comedian, radio broadcaster, author, and campaigner from England. Russell is a spiritual man who enjoys assisting people. He expressed his happiness by saying that he is pleased when he is good to others. He also thinks that we all have a "higher self," and he practices Meditation and yoga daily.

LMFAO

"You are luring into your life whatever you are envisioning."

LMFAO is an American electronic dance music duo of Redfoo and SkyBlu, uncle and nephew. In interviews, they've said they're fascinated with the book "The Secret." They trust the

Law of Attraction and frequently employ it to achieve their goals. "I'm in Miami," one of the songs, was composed before they had even visited Miami; they were expressing it. LMFAO use the Law of Attraction, visualization, and manifestation to attain their goals.

Conor McGregor

"I picture good things all the time. I imagine triumph, success, and plenty of it all the time. It's all occurring because I envisioned it." Conor Anthony McGregor is a champion boxer and mixed martial artist from Ireland. He is presently contracted to the Ultimate Fighting Championships. He is the current UFC Lightweight Champion and has previously held the UFC Featherweight Championship. He has stated that he used visualization and the Law of Attraction. He claims that visualizing his aspirations and aims has aided him in achieving them. He envisioned his achievements, especially winning the UFC belt, till it became a reality.

Jon Jones

"I trust in the Law of Attraction and that you may create things with your words. And I think that once you know where you're going and what you need, the Universe will find a way to make room for you." Jonathan Dwight Jones is a three-time and present Heavyweight Champion of the Ultimate Fighting Championship, who won the championship in 2011 and 2017 and the interim title in 2016. He believes in the Law of Attraction and that you may manifest your desires by speaking them into existence. Before his bout in 2011, he signed his name as "Champ 2011" before receiving the title.

Misty May-Treanor and Kerri Walsh

"Visualization is a big part of what we do. To be ready to obtain the views, sounds, pressure, and excitement will be extremely beneficial to us in the future." American Olympic volleyball gold medalists Kerri Walsh and Misty May-Treanor have won three gold medals. They've indicated that visualization, yoga, and meditation have assisted them in accomplishing and staying concentrated during their successful professions. In a conversation with USA TODAY, they discussed visualization and how it assists them to remain focused and moving forward.

Lindsey Vonn

"I always picture what I'm going to do before I execute it. By the time I get at the starting line, I've already raced the race 100 times in my thoughts, visualizing how I'll handle the turns." Lindsey Caroline Vonn is a member of the US Ski Team and a World Cup alpine ski racer. She is one of only 2 women skiers who have won 4 World Cup overall titles. Lindsey has stated that she frequently employs visualization when it comes to competing. She also employs visualization methods before races, which she claims gives her a "competitive advantage."

Deepthi's Story

"My name is Deepthi, and I'm writing to share how I could manifest my vacation plans to the United States after enrolling in Personal Mentorship using the LOA created by my mentor, Mr. Rajesh Vairapandian."

"I had always loved to travel to my brother in the United States, and I had a lot of preparations in place to help pay for my trip, but something was missing."

"After attending this course and receiving comprehensive mentoring from Mr. Rajesh, I was able to manifest my visit not just to the United States to see my brother but even to several other wonderful locations so effortlessly and at no cost!!"

"My headquarters summoned me on a visit, and they paid for the entire journey!!"

"I flew Emirates first class and stayed in the most costly and luxurious hotels possible, and it was an incredible trip."

"I had always planned a one-week vacation to the United States, but after following my mentor's advice and doing many simple techniques, I was able to manifest my vacation for a whole month!!!"

"I owe Mr. Rajesh a huge debt of gratitude for his incredible mentorship and direction in helping all of us achieve our objectives and ambitions in such a short period."

"I advise you to learn the Law of Attraction for that experience and allow you time to explore so many beautiful things!!"

Tameka's Story

"When I was 13 years old, my grandparents called my two siblings and me down and informed us that they didn't have enough money to buy us anything at all on Christmas that year. We were respectful about it, but we still wanted to experience the joy that every youngster craves. I went to my bedroom after receiving the updates and lay there wondering, I understood, yet the inner part of me was also heartbroken. Without realizing what would occur next, I began to recall my other grandma and aunt from my father's side. I knew exactly what I needed and how I would get it. My idea was to come and offer $200 to each of my brothers and me. I could picture them handing it in our palms and the excitement we were experiencing at the time."

"My doorbell rang not even 15 minutes after I had that idea. My father's grandmother and grandfather were on their way to pick me up with my brothers and take us shopping. When we arrived at the stores, they halted and handed each of us $200, telling us to buy anything we wanted. I realized something was going on and that I had formed a connection at that time, and it happened to me more and more depending on what I asked for and how I requested and felt. I felt compelled to spread the wonderful news."

Conclusion

YOU SUCCEEDED! THIS BOOK WAS COMPLETELY DONE BY YOU! You're well on your way to creating the lifestyle you've always imagined. I know it looks strange to think about, but you will indeed enjoy a life that is far beyond your wildest dreams. Conceding your mind to the process, altering your mentality and thought processes, and welcoming in what you desire and deserve in life are all part of the Law of Attraction as well as the manifestation process.

Remember, it's all about making it happen, experiencing it, and loving it. Our energy and mood grow without us doing anything when we submit our emotions and enable ourselves the opportunity to create a life that we are ecstatic about!

Imagine how quickly you'll be able to manifest your goals if you use what you've acquired here and implement it in life, maintaining your thoughts optimistic and in a high vibrational state. The best part is allowing yourself to appreciate and embrace this novel approach to being, living, and thinking.

Never, ever question your ability to make your aspirations a reality. The self-improvement effort you accomplish with the guidance of this book will last your entire life.

Congratulations.

"Download your Manifesting Journal here"